FILLING UP YOUR THINK TANK

Bill Stearns

VICTOR BOOKS

A DIVISION OF SCRIPTURE PRESS PUBLICATIONS INC.
USA CANADA ENGLAND

▶ This book is designed to help you make the most of your mind. You can read it by yourself or study it with the help of a group. Student activity booklets (Rip-Offs) and a leader's guide with visual aids (SonPower Multiuse Transparency Masters) are available from your local Christian bookstore or from the publisher.

All Bible quotations, unless otherwise indicated, are from the *New American Standard Bible,* © the Lockman Foundation 1960, 1962, 1963, 1968, 1971, 1972, 1973, 1975, 1977.

Library of Congress Catalog Card Number: 85-62703
ISBN: 0-89693-264-8

Recommended Dewey Decimal Classification: 248.83
Suggested Subject Heading: YOUTH-RELIGIOUS LIFE

Contents

The man behind the convenience-store counter looked like Winston Churchill. "No, I don't believe we carry Supercorn Sweeties. It's a cereal, you say?"

"Yeah," I said. "They've got a Cosmic Heroes Space-copter in the box. Of course, it's not for me." I opened a freezer and took out a Fudgesicle.

"Of course," he said. "Do you realize you have a stripe of mud or something up your back?"

"Oh." I checked my back. "Yeah. Rode through a field where they had the sprinklers on. Got any writers' magazines?"

"You're a writer." He nodded. "Then why do you have blue tissues stuffed up your nostrils? I thought maybe you were a pest control worker."

"Oh, I forgot about those. And I just remembered I forgot to lock up John outside. How much for the fudge bar?"

"You usually lock John up?"

I smiled winningly. "I call my bike John."

"I see. The fudge bar is forty-one cents. And just what is it that you're writing?"

The Think Tank in your Head

"Ah, well, books. A book. I'm writing a book on how to think."

He began to grin and pinched the bridge of his nose to control it. "How to think," he said. "You?" He gestured at my bare feet, cut-offs, and mud-striped T-shirt. "You're writing a book on. . . ."

"Well, Einstein flunked fourth grade, you know. So I figure there's hope for all of us." I smiled, dropped my change so it rolled off the counter, bashed into the glass door as I tried to exit through the "in" side, and the Fudgesicle tumbled down my leg. Outside, I tripped over a newspaper stand and fell headlong into John. I glanced through the window and Winston Churchill was laughing hysterically. I poked my head back in and admitted, "Well, hope for most of us, anyway."

• • •

But now that I'm safely back at my typewriter, I'll restate it: There's hope for *all* of us. I don't care how air-headed you think you are, you can become one of the world's greatest thinkers.

Remember the old *Kung Fu* TV series in which young Grasshopper grew, lesson-by-lesson, into a tough, sensitive, wise warrior—a hero who understood what was important in life? Well, that can be you—regardless of what the world thinks, regardless of your grades, regardless of what's been going on in your head lately.

Maybe you've been thinking about the free enterprise system or blueberry-and-liverpaste sandwiches or Andromeda or bodies or "The Battle Hymn of the Republic" or fullbacks or drawbacks or sore backs or the police or The Police or fungi or suntans or. . . .

There's a lot of thinking going on. Envision it. There are thousands of people like you reading these words, and all their heads have been thinking about thousands—millions—of different things.

As a junior higher I stumbled around wide-eyed one day when I finally, clearly realized that the snot-nosed kid beside me had a whole life going on inside his head—a whole universe of thoughts and feelings with him at the center of it. Just like every other kid and every adult. Billions of people bumbling through their own little schedules are at this instant thinking non-stop about every bitty detail of their lives, about conversations they'd had or would have, about greased bearings and love and tomorrow and murder and God and the moon and pain. Right now some of them are even thinking about you. Thinking gets a little cosmic, right?

Well, I'll try to keep our study on thinking from getting too cosmic. In fact, you'll be surprised how practical, how everyday-life-changing thinking about thinking can be. I'll try to keep you awake as I toss out some new things to think about—new *input*. But the input is only the beginning, since *how* you think and the ways you *use* that thinking in your life are also big factors in your becoming one of the world's greatest thinkers. Visualize those three components:

INPUT	THOUGHT PATTERNS	LIFE PATTERNS

THINKING ABOUT THINKING

God thought up the way your mind works. He knows how a brain should run, and His Word is adamant on the care and feeding of your mental faculties for optimum brain operations. The fact that your thinking is vital stuff gets to be pretty obvious as you look up "mind" or "think" in a Bible concordance. You'll find dozens of passages that teach us:

▶ God has a mind.

▶ There's a tie-in between mind and emotions, as in the phrases "sorrow of mind."

▶ Our minds are the key to personal peace.

▶ Minds can be doubtful, ready, humble, vain, reprobate, willing, fervent, feeble, corrupted, blind, defiled, sober, double, faint, or pure.

▶ The mind can be God's enemy.

▶ Being like-minded is essential to fellowship.

▶ We can enjoy unshaken, sound minds.

▶ We're to learn to love God with our minds.

▶ Our minds can be renewed to become like Christ's.

▶ We can have the mind of God.

We'll be discussing a lot of these biblical thoughts on thoughts. But for now, to get a grip on where *your* head is these days, ask yourself, "Is God more interested in my actions or my thinking? Is He really thinking about little old me all the time? Can He change my thinking if I don't want Him to? Would I like to be wise?"

Thinking is strange. We really don't know much about it. Do you think only in your brain? How is thinking different from feeling? Is there any limit to ideas? Are phenomena like extrasensory perception or mental telepathy ordinary powers of the original brain? How do animals think? What is consciousness?

But I'm getting cosmic and spacey again. Let's just say thinking is intriguing, wonderful stuff. It's unlimited. (I mean, somebody actually thought for hours and hours designing something as incredible as the 1893 Chicago World's Fair agricultural highlight: a life-size horse and mounted knight made entirely of prunes!

Think of it!) Think how amazing it is that you can be completely occupied with thoughts that nobody on earth suspects you of having!

Thinking is nonstop. You think all the time, right? Either your thoughts are your own—clear, verbalized, vague, or intuitive—or you think somebody else's thoughts. When I need you to think of a black cat, I send my thoughts to you in words. Imagine a black cat curled up, licking a paw, then playing with its tail, then glaring with yellow eyes up at you. See? It works; you can think my thoughts.

When you understand and state the Pythagorean theorem, you think Pythagoras' centuries-old thoughts. When you play Bartok's *New World Symphony* on your kazoo, you're indirectly thinking his thoughts. When you unthinkingly adopt your parents' attitudes toward another race, their thoughts are in your head just as much as your own thoughts. When you understand and memorize Bible verses, you think God's thoughts.

But regardless of whose thoughts bump around in your mind, thinking is a time-consuming occupation. You can sneak out a window at night to get away from your family, or cultivate garlic-breath to get away from friends and enemies alike, but you can never get away from your mind.

Whether on a subconscious or a conscious level, your mind is always working. Some psychologists call this full-time thinking "brain chatter." Literary types call the written form of it "stream of consciousness." When it's broadcast from Zelda Hosehead's voicebox, it's called running off at the mouth. But think about it: You think twenty-four hours a day, year after year until you die—and afterward forever, according to the Bible.

Do you ever enjoy just letting your mind run, watching the images and ideas that constantly parade through your gray matter? Close your eyes right now and notice the first two things that pop—seemingly unbidden—into your mind. Whether you think you've got the IQ of a potato or the logic of Mr. Spock, realize that you constantly do a lot of data-stream thinking!

Thinking sometimes is a drag. Every once in a while brain chatter gets irritating—as when you're *trying* to fall asleep and your mind keeps replaying annoying scenes and conversations. Ever feel that you're losing your marbles, that your thinking is running away with you? You grab the sides of your head, roll your eyes, and say,"I gotta stop thinking these things . . .!" Well, don't feel like the Lone Ranger. Handling what goes on in our heads is a very fine art for all of us. Thinking is tough to control.

SLOWING DOWN THE CHATTER

"It's like I want to quit thinking for a while." Allen had microwaved all his albums and unraveled his tapes when last summer's camp speaker had convinced him that *all* secular music is Satanic. Now, months later, Al missed it.

"I used to go into my room and plug in the headphones, sometimes look at a magazine; it was like my own private space in the music. Didn't have to worry about my face or geometry or Dad's drinking or anything. Know what I mean, Stearns?"

"Yeah, I know the feeling. I'd blast my car radio whan I was driving cross-country, just cruising along with the music. I wouldn't even realize I'd driven for hours without worrying about how long the drive would be. What's your mom do to let her brain rest from brain chatter?"

"Hmmm. Probably TV."

"Your dad?"

"That's easy. Johnny Walker Red."

"Your English teacher?"

"I think he's a classical music fiend. Reads poetry.

Weird."

"The preacher?"

"Probably prays. *My* head runs away with me when I try to pray." Al's eyes lit up. "Maybe he reads the Bible. Would that slow down brain chatter? Like help me quit thinking what I don't want to think?"

"Do your gym socks stink?"

"I guess the answer is yes, huh? Well, what about my music?"

That's a topic we'll get to later. But realize for now that people work pretty hard to stop thinking—with music, reading, games, TV, movies, physical activities, dope, booze, even suicide. People want to avoid thinking about pain or trouble or humiliation—past, present, future—because thinking about troubling stuff troubles us.

When you think depressing thoughts, you feel depressed; you act depressed. When you think exciting thoughts, you feel excited and act excited. And the same for confusing thoughts, happy thoughts, angry thoughts, etc. We often want to stop our brain-chatter thinking because it *affects* us. Brilliant observation, eh? But we're getting to something here: How you *think* directly affects the way you *feel*, the way you *act*, the way you *are* as a person.

YOU ARE WHAT YOU THINK

Are you a rabid philatelist? An agnostic? An egghead? A conservative? A Democrat, feminist, terrorist, video-game fiend, speed-demon, anti-nuker, Girl Scout, philodendron-lover, failure, Christian, Dallas Cowboys fan, a good kid? You became these things as a result of your *thinking*. Your thinking *shapes* you.

You become what you think is the basic principle in thinking about thinking. The Bible records, "As [a person] thinks within himself, so he is" (Proverbs 23:7).

That is, if you pick up true *input* that allows your mind to crank out dazzling, true *thought patterns*, you'll begin developing dazzling and true *life patterns!* And if you practice second-hand, full-of-baloney thought patterns based on second-hand, full-of-baloney input, it's not too hard to guess what your lifestyle will eventually be like.

Now, notice that God doesn't hold to the simplistic scare tactic employed by some people—that whatever you see or hear automatically makes you into what you'll be. Thank the Lord, "Garbage In" (nasty input) doesn't have to equal "Garbage Out" (nasty lifestyle). This GIGO principle is for machines, not human believers.

God says you become what you *think*, not just what you're exposed to. (You don't have to become a pervert just because you overheard a dirty joke today.) But we'll cover all that later. The important thing is recognizing the process (illustrated below).

INPUT ◊ THOUGHT PATTERNS ◊ LIFE PATTERNS

For example, if you get constant input such as, "You're stupid, kid" and you start thinking that you're stupid, you will be. You'll avoid everything that demands brains, and you'll let yourself fail tests because you decided beforehand that you don't have enough intelligence.

If you constantly feed on scary stories of attacks and robberies and murders and kidnapping, you'll begin to think life offers nothing but fear. And you'll act accordingly paranoid: mistrusting every stranger, never attempting anything that isn't absolutely safe.

If your scale of rating people tells you that Farley

Twoshoes rates a -3 in appearance and a -117 in personality, eventually you'll snub good old Farley, to his face or behind his back.

If you think Christianity is a game to force good behavior on people, eventually Christianity will be just a game to you. You'll show your true thoughts—maybe when you get out on your own—by living life patterns that deny the spiritual value of Christian discipleship.

If you think the wild life is all it's cracked up to be, in the long run you'll get around to trying it out.

If you think most people are better than you, you'll become withdrawn—not learning new skills, seldom practicing social graces with new people. And so most people *will* get better than you at most things.

If you think you have no power to resist temptations, you won't—since you just give in each time without a fight, planning on losing anyway.

Get it? You'll become what you think.

THINKING IS BETTER THAN SNAKE OIL

Since you become what you think, you can consider this study as a great brain-change operation. I'll try every trick in the Book to stuff your head with some true-type input, to guide you in some exercises for renewed thought patterns. Then you get to watch the changes that start cropping up in your life as you:

▶ gain confidence in your appearance and poise,
▶ find you're no longer a slave to sensual lust,
▶ understand yourself better,
▶ don't worry much anymore,
▶ get to be closer friends with God,
▶ have the discipline to do what's good for your mind and body,
▶ anticipate the future with enthusiasm,
▶ practice patience with family members,
▶ don't feel so kicked around by emotional moods,

▶ get on top of your money needs and dreams,
▶ handle your hassles, heartaches, and pain with strength,
▶ live out the life God created you for,
▶ leave your mark on the world.

Sounds like a list of snakeoil or mail-order ad claims, doesn't it? People pay big bucks to learn self-confidence, or how to snag love relationships, or handle finances. But for you, my friend, they're free! These free benefits come automatically when your input is truth and when the God of truth coaches your thought patterns. When you learn to think about life the way God does—to think God's thoughts—life fits together *well.*

2

It's time to give your old brain a little workout. See how you do on the following Mental Obstacle Course. Be sure to finish each brainteaser as well as you can since you'll be referring to your findings later on. Get help on these if you'd like; don't put any pressure on yourself since there are no right or wrong answers to any of the questions. Relax and let these exercises challenge your thinking.

OBSTACLE #1
"Therefore I have declared that which I did not understand; things too wonderful for me, which I did not know" (Job 42:3).

In Thailand, biologist C.R. Carpenter studied a tribe of gibbons that sing in chorus every morning to the rising sun. The monkeys scamper to the top of a huge tree and start singing an E note in unison. Then they raise the pitch in half steps, louder at each note change, as the sun rises above the horizon. Before each new note, they toss in a "grace note" of the original E

Mind Games

pitch. When they've sung an entire octave, arriving at an E again, they break for a moment of absolute silence, then swing down through the branches to begin their day.

What questions come to your mind about this strange animal activity? Does it bother you in some way?

_____

_____

_____

What new thought(s) does this suggest to you?

_____

_____

_____

OBSTACLE #2

"Man does not know his time" (Ecclesiastes 9:12).

If you could be healthy right to the end, would you like to live to be 100? How about 125 years? With ideal health, physical strength, and clarity of mind, you could pack a lot of living into 125 years, right? How about 150 years of physical and mental health? Think of the careers you could explore in that double-length lifetime, the smarts you'd pick up even learning things the hard way all those years! Think of how many good people you'd meet.

What would it be like to be 200 years old?! 500 years? (Tough to stretch your imagination that far, right?) 1000 years? Think of the wisdom you'd gain in over ten times the normal life span. Imagine the projects you could accomplish. "Yeah, I think I'll build a toothpick replica of the city of London; it'll only take me 120 years or so." Think how good you'd get at racquetball!

Don't lose the feeling of this. Push your thinking to visualize what it would be like to live a happy, healthy, and mentally alert life span of 2,000 years. How about 5,000 years? (Does not compute very realistically in your head, right? Well, *work* at it; try to feel the perspective of somebody who's lived since the height of the early Sumerian civilization in 3000 B.C.)

Now, let's get really crazy. How would you like to live a healthy 100,000 years? A million years? Try to visualize the time of a million years on a *distance* scale. Let's say you're hiking from Los Angeles to Albuquerque, or from New York City to Louisville, Kentucky. That's about 1,000 kilometers. If that distance represented a million years, one stride would represent a year gone by. Think how many strides you would take in that distance!

Only a tiny segment of each stride (the length of this dash [—]) would equal a full 24-hour day. Think how many days you would experience in a *million years*! (Are you hearing Twilight Zone music yet?) How about living a billion years? A trillion healthy years?

Well, as a person who receives God's gift of everlasting life in Christ, you are *actually* going to live for billions and trillions of years! (Although we won't be counting, right? I mean, all those birthday candles. . . .)

In what ways does the actuality of living for more than trillions of years affect your feelings about the next 45 minutes? About having to work a few hours tomorrow? About getting all the gusto you can for yourself while you're young?

_____

_____

_____

_____

_____

What do you *think* about living forever? (comments, doubts, questions, etc.)

_____

_____

_____

_____

OBSTACLE #3

"I advise you to buy from Me . . . eyesalve to anoint your eyes that you may see" (Revelation 3:18).
   What do you see?

Two different images in the same drawing, right? Now *tell* your brain that your eyes are looking at a white vase while you stare at the drawing for 30 seconds. What happens? What does this suggest to you about how your mind can handle contradictions? (two contrasting things being true at the same time)

_____

_____

What determines what you see—your senses or your mind?

_____

_____

Can you successfully tell your mind to ignore what's real once you've seen it?

_____

The 15th-century astronomer, Galileo, stated, "A discovery of the sense cannot err." But how precise are your senses? What does this drawing tell you about how much your mind can trust your senses?

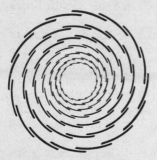

Is this a nest of spirals or circles?

OBSTACLE #4

"Consider the work of God (Ecclesiastes 7:13).

What do you think? Is Christianity having a big impact on today's world?　　☐ Yes　　☐ No

Think through the following statistics, then jot down your well-educated opinion:

▶ For the first time in history there are now Christians and Christian churches in every inhabited country on earth.

▶ The editors of *The World Christian Encyclopedia* judge that Christians are more active in sharing Christ than in previous generations. Averaged out, each Christian in the world is evangelizing 2.4 times more non-Christians now than in 1900.

▶ Every *day* sees a worldwide increase of about 78,000 new Christians.

▶ Every *week* approximately 1,000 new churches are established in Asia and Africa alone.

▶ South America has been characterized by phenomenal church growth recently. One church in Santiago has over 90,000 members; another in Sao Paul can seat 25,000 at a single service.

▶ In Africa, only 9 percent of the population was Christian in 1900. In the year 2000, nearly 50 percent of that continent's population will be Christian.

▶ The largest gathering of humans in history was a Christian meeting held in 1980 in Seoul, South Korea with a crowd of 2,700,000!

▶ In South Korea, each day welcomes the start of six new churches.

▶ One church in South Korea has a half million members, with over 19,000 home Bible study groups.

▶ Though persecuted for decades, the number of Christians in the communist People's Republic of China is estimated to be between 30 million and 50 million believers!

▶ C. Peter Wagner, author of *On the Crest of the*

Wave (source of these stats), says, "When we lift up our eyes to what God is doing worldwide today, that early activity around the eastern Mediterranean seems like a small pilot project compared to what is happening now!"

Well, in the last couple minutes, has your thinking changed? What do you think *now* about Christianity's impact on the world today?

_____

_____

_____

OBSTACLE #5

"Who . . . has given understanding to the mind?" (Job 38:36)

Do inorganic (nonliving, as in gold nuggets, magnetic force, aluminum pop-top rings, etc.) things ever design and make organic (living or once-living such as peanuts or cowhide or people) things?

_____

Do organic things ever design and make inorganic things?

_____

Do things *without* minds ever design and make things *with* minds?

_____

Check the correct diagram of what you know about the world:

☐ **A.** **MINDLESS THINGS ⟡ MIND**

☐ **B.** **MIND ⟡ MINDLESS THINGS**

What does this tell you about the beginnings of life in the universe?

_____

_____

_____

OBSTACLE #6
"Much study is a weariness" (Ecclesiastes 12:12, KJV).

Sometimes it takes a disgusting amount of effort to think about something. Even past the point when you decide that you won't be able to figure it out, determine now to gut it out.

Put your brain to work finding the symmetrical, five-pointed star (like the stars in the American flag) in the following drawing. And, no, I haven't included the answer on the back page somewhere; you'll have to work at it on your own. Good luck and congratulations when you finally find it!

There's certainly plenty more to think about than just the stuff in that little mental pop quiz. But take a brain-wave reading right now. How did you feel about having to think about each item, to concentrate without your old brain chatter running away with your thoughts? Especially since I wasn't standing over you with a spike-studded yardstick or threatening you with a failing grade in a course, wasn't it hard to actually force yourself to *think*? Didn't it wear you out? Did it

spark your curiosity and yet almost make you mad? The
effort it takes to really think something through guarantees that "Ten All-Expense-Paid Days to Think" won't
be the most popular game-show prize.

GET BRAIN-TOUGH
Henry Ford said, "Thinking is the hardest work there
is, which is probably why so few engage in it!" A lot of
people are uneasy about thinking hard because they
think only upper-intelligence-level people can think.
Or maybe they're just flat out lazy. Others don't want
to be led beyond their depth by thinking something
through; they might have to change their minds about
some long-cherished idea. It's like the guy who says,
"My mind's made up. Don't confuse me with the
facts!"

Christians often go in for easy answers instead of personally struggling with tough thinking, with serious doubts and questions. Many simply repeat what they've heard about profound or controversial subjects since parroting unquestioned dogma is easier than thinking an issue through. Abortion? "Well, my minister says. . . ." Christian rock music? "My Sunday School teacher always said. . . ." Reincarnation? "Well, my parents say. . . ."

Ignorance is sometimes considered cool. I've known all kinds of straight-A students who feel they have to apologize whenever they're forced to admit how hard they study.

Christians sometimes frown on thinking because it's considered to be the opposite of faith. "Don't think, just believe" is prevalent advice. One best-selling Christian author suggests that in order to see God work, Christians need to pack their brains into little boxes and shoot them all to the moon. But is it unspiritual to figure out truth? Do we have to be stupid to be good Christians? Is it dangerous to do some original thinking instead of just mimicking what every other Christian says?

The problem with this down-with-thinking attitude is that it misreads "For the mind set on the flesh is hostile toward God" (Romans 8:7), as "For the mind is hostile toward God." There's a big difference between the two. No, we don't have to understand—and can't understand—all spiritual truths, but that's certainly no reason to quit thinking altogether.

USING YOUR HEAD

Yes, the natural mind—the "mind set on the flesh"—and its way of thinking doesn't rate in God's universe. "Where is the wise man . . . of this age? Has not God made foolish the wisdom of the world?" (1 Corinthians

1:20) And it's obvious that world-class thinkers can be bimbos, "always learning and never able to come to the knowledge of the truth" (2 Timothy 3:7) when it comes to universe-class wisdom. So we won't waste time with the natural thinking "of this age . . . of the world."

But don't get on the bandwagon to ban *super*-natural thinking! Read the whole context of 1 Corinthians 1 and realize that "Christ Jesus . . . became to us *wisdom*" (1:30). Take on God's command to think about His kind of input (Philippians 4:8) and to "think with straight thinking" (literal wording in Romans 12:3). Become a mastermind of God's wisdom as constantly urged in His Word—such as in Proverbs:

▶ "Know wisdom." (Proverbs 1:2)
▶ "Acquire wisdom." (4:5)
▶ "Give attention to wisdom." (5:1)
▶ "Discern wisdom." (8:5)
▶ "Get wisdom and instruction and understanding." (23:23)

Christians are commanded to use their heads.

Notice that these injunctions to wise up are for anybody, regardless of IQ. This is good news, folks. Remember when I said there was hope for *all* of us? Even if you're ground-level intelligence in your natural thinking—you're a poor student or only "average" or "bad in reading," etc.—you can become one of the world's greatest thinkers! You'll have more insight than all of your teachers (Psalm 119:99). Even if you're a simpleton, rejoice: You can be made wise (Psalm 19:7). *You don't need intelligence to think wisely and well.*

So get strange. Think. Take responsibility for your own brainworks. Don't leave the care and feeding of your mind, and consequently of your life, to well-meaning parents, teachers, ministers, or Christian writers. You're not going to blaze a life of success and wisdom by letting everybody else do your thinking for you. Wisdom is nontransferable.

So in the middle of all the nonstop brain chatter that shapes your life, determine now to become a tough, sensitive and wise warrior who understands life. Be one of that rare breed: the thinking Christian.

3

If it took a team of seven researchers and a lab full of computers three years to analyze the 23-neuron nervous system of a worm, how long would it take them to analyze your 10 billion-neuron brain?

You got it. It'll never happen. Some scientists think of the brain as the final frontier since there's still so much to understand about what goes on in our heads. Among the mysteries:

▶ How can a pea-sized gram of brain tissue contain the communication capability of the whole world's telephone system?

▶ How can the brain record up to 1,000 pieces of information per second from birth to death?

▶ How can the brain monitor more than 100,000 chemical reactions each second?

You can wow over all those exciting brain tidbits in your biology or physiology books, right? We're not so much concerned right now with examining your gray matter. Our study will focus on you *mind*, not your brain.

Is there a difference?

Have You Lost Your Mind Lately?

YOUR MIND/YOUR BRAIN

In 1961 a young South African patient lay on a cold operating table with electrode wires attached to a single contact point in the temporal lobe of his brain. Canadian neurosurgeon Wilder Penfield flipped on the current, and the patient began describing the sights, smells, and sounds of his home country. The electrode stimulated the brain to reexperience a memory "stored" at that location.

"It was astonishing to him to realize," said Dr. Penfield, "that he was laughing with his friends on a farm in South Africa, while he was also fully conscious of being in the operating room in Montreal."

The experiment brought up a nearly philosophical question: If the brain, stimulated by the electrode, made the patient aware of the South African scene, then *what* made him aware in Montreal of his awareness of the South African scene? If the brain is "watching" a memory, there must be something *else* watching the brain watching the memory.

In another experiment, Dr. Penfield placed an electrode in a motor area of a patient's brain cortex. "I challenged him to keep his hand from moving when the electrode was applied," said Dr. Penfield. "He seized it with the other hand and struggled to hold it still. Thus one hand, under the control of the right hemisphere of the brain driven by an electrode, and the other hand which he controlled through the left hemisphere, struggled against each other." Dr. Penfield concluded, "Behind the brain action of one hemisphere was the electrode. Behind the action of the other hemisphere was the patient's *mind*."

Dr. Penfield's conclusion that the mind is not part of the brain isn't a popular scientific view, as he points out in his book *The Mystery of the Mind*. Most twentieth-century scientists have believed thinking results from electro-chemical reactions and the illusion of a "mind" can be explained by what happens in your brain.

Carl Ludwig, Emil du-Bois-Reyman, and Hermann von Helmholtz—three giants in the scientific world of the 1800s—issued a *Manifesto* that still affects the thinking of modern scientific minds: "All the activities of living material, including consciousness, are ultimately to be explained in terms of physics and chemistry." In other words, your mind *is* your brain.

BEHIND THE MIND = BRAIN THEORY
There are two driving forces behind the mind = brain theory: empiricism and evolution.

Empiricism says you know things only through what your senses or scientific instruments can record. By the late 1800s most educated people believed that non-physical things—such as spirit or mind—which couldn't be seen, heard, felt, tasted, smelled, or measured, shouldn't be considered a part of reality.

Evolution, meanwhile, was a powerful force that said the man on the street evolved as an extension of lower forms of animal life. So if the man on the street insisted he had a mind, that mind was just an evolved extension of his brain.

Empiricism made man just physical. *Evolution* made him just animal. These beliefs were the basis of study into man's nature. Psychologists believed everything about human beings could be explained by their physical characteristics. Scientists felt they could easily experiment with animals and apply the findings to humans. They relied heavily on animal brain research to figure out man's mind.

JUST A MATERIAL WORLD?
It's still taught that your mind is just an extension of your brain. This view that the mind and brain are one

thing is called the *monistic* view of man.

MIND = BRAIN OR MIND = MATTER

Monism is popular because it's so simple. A human being is just one unified thing—a thing that composes symphonies, steals bases, and configures printer microbuffers, sure. But basically you're viewed as an evolving, physical piece of matter. So you can be studied the way matter is studied—scientifically. If science can find out what makes you tick, science can make you better. It can fix you. Ultimately, science can control you, because you're really no more than a glorified machine without a soul.

But monism has not always been with us. In fact, monism is a new kid on the block compared to the view of man's nature called *dualism*. Dualism is the view that man is made up of two basic entities—one material and the other nonmaterial.

MIND = NONMATERIAL
BRAIN = MATTER

Dualism was popular in the time of the ancient Greeks, who thought of the body as the prisonhouse of the mind or *psyche*—which is often also translated into English as *soul*.

Rene Descartes, the philosopher-scientist, topped the 1600s international charts with the smash hit "Cogito, Ergo Sum." (I think, therefore I am.) He said the nonmaterial mind acted on the body through the brain. He made mind and brain dependent on each other as a fountain pen and ink are; the pen won't write without ink and the ink can't say anything without the pen.

Descartes' dualism was popular in his day because everybody and his grandmother believed in the nonmaterial dimension, the supernatural. The material body and brain were created, the nonmaterial mind or soul was created, and the two somehow interacted.

But by the 1800s, scientists were generally skeptical of Descartes' dualism. Dualism raises some obvious questions such as, *"Exactly* how does a nonmaterial spirit or soul interact with a material brain?" and "Who creates these things?" So it's easy to see why modern scientists who generally aren't crazy about creationism aren't crazy about dualism. If you admit there is a nonmaterial mind or soul, you have to explain its origin. And that's where you get into spiritual, supernatural things. These things are undetectable by the senses or instruments, therefore they're very unscientific.

A new dualism is slowly emerging among researchers in various fields involving man's mind. New evidence from brain research, parapsychology, and physics in the last 30 years is making a lot of scientists think twice about dualism.

Dr. Penfield's experiments, for instance, have presented evidence that the brain isn't all there is to man's self-consciousness. In *The Mystery of the Mind* he writes, "For my own part, after years of striving to explain the mind on the basis of the brain acting alone, I have come to the conclusion that it is simpler (and far easier to be logical) if one adopts the hypothesis that our being does consist of *two* fundamental elements."

The new worlds of quantum physics and relativity have also pushed many scientists back to a dualistic view of mind and matter. Warner Heisenberg's studies early in this century emphasized that atoms—which used to be called the "building blocks of the universe"—are not material things at all. Albert Einstein developed his nuclear theories on the basis that on the atomic level, the "physical" properties of space and time do not exist.

Physicists have had to acknowledge that although the

subatomic particles called neutrinos have no mass, no electrical charge, no magnetic fields, and although they're not affected by gravity, electrical forces, or magnetic forces, they exist. Physicists are increasingly aware of the nonphysical nature of the universe.

The more science frankly admits about its studies of man, the more obvious it becomes that we're not just physical animals. There's something more, something called by many philosophers "the ghost in the machine." The view of man that fits the newest research goes back thousands of years before Descartes, before the ancient Greeks, to a dualistic view of man as seen by his Maker.

WHAT GOES ON IN YOUR HEART/MIND/SOUL /SPIRIT?

I hope you didn't nod off during that quick philosophy-history session, because this isn't some academic discussion we're having. We're talking about *you*. What makes up you? Are you a hodgepodge of nerve endings and chemical reactions? Or a ghost bouncing around in a machine? Or a breathing computer? Or a material girl in a material world? Where do your brain's electrical impulses end and thinking begin? Are your thoughts limited to your head?

The Bible describes you as having three "parts"—a nonmaterial spirit and soul and a material body. (See 1 Thessalonians 5:23.) Elsewhere, biblical writers suggest you're made up of only two parts—one material and the other nonmaterial. (See Matthew 10:28.)

But putting the two descriptions together isn't too tough even for us nontheologians. Think of yourself as a nonmaterial human spirit and a material human body. Where the two realities overlap, you get a third part: your soul.

Think through the next diagram. Notice the inter-

SPIRITUAL INPUT
▼

SPIRIT
Center of being,
of awareness of God,
of *the will*

SOUL
Center of thinking,
of self-awareness,
of emotions,
of *the mind or heart.*

BODY
Center of biochemical reactions,
of awareness of others,
of *the brain.*

▲
SENSORY INPUT

action of your body with its brain and your soul with its mind and heart. It's pretty obvious that the body affects the mind. Bite your thumb and see what your mind says! And the mind affects the body. For instance, it's been estimated that 80 percent of sports performance is determined mentally, not just physically.

The way you think also affects your health. "The health of our minds can profoundly affect the health of our bodies," said Bruce Hensel, M.D., in a syndicated newspaper article. "Tension can lead to headaches and worry can aggravate ulcers. And more and more, scientists are finding that mental attitude may also play a major role in our susceptibility to diseases like cancer."

The body-soul link is obvious, but it's a little harder to realize that your *spirit* also interacts with your soul. We'll see in our upcoming studies that your spirit's *will* is constantly involved with your soul's *mind* and *heart*.

Check the diagram again and notice that while the physical senses provide input through your brain to your mind, the spirit also brings input to your mind from the spiritual dimension.

Centered in the soul, your mind as described in the Bible includes both mental and emotional aspects. *Nous* and *dianoia* are the original Greek words for *mind* in the New Testament. *Nous* describes your faculty of knowing, reasoning, and judging. *Dianoia* suggests meditation, a thinking through of something. Notice how these words are used in passages such as Matthew 22:37, Romans 1:28, and Titus 1:15.

Kardea is the word which is often translated *heart*. *Kardea* describes your faculty for grief, joy, desires, conscience, and affection. The word is used in verses such as John 14:1, Acts 21:13, Ephesians 5:19, and 1 John 3:20. Don't worry about trying to keep these terms exactly straight, because often the English Bible uses *spirit*, *soul*, *heart*, and *mind* all to describe the same thing—the inner you.

The mind is pretty slippery to define. Your heart-mind is tricky (Jeremiah 17:9). You may notice your share of conflicting thoughts and feelings. (Here I go, leaping up to run six miles. But then again, *Leave It to Beaver* is just coming on and the chocolate-chocolate chip ice cream in the refrigerator is calling to me!) Your mind works on conscious levels and in the sub-conscious which is beneath your level of awareness.

Whole libraries have complied a mind-boggling amount of information on the ways and workings of your mind. But we're going to keep things simple by taking a quick look at three "levels" of your mind.

THOUGHTS, ATTITUDES, AND BELIEFS
Your awesome brain controls the basic involuntary activity of your body, right? It doesn't take an act of your

mind to say, "Breathe," every time you want a lung to suck in oxygen. But every other action of your body requires your *will* to work through your *mind* and *brain* to stimulate your *body* to act.

When you first learned to walk, or pull off a half-gainer, or say "hippopotamus," or kiss, your mind had to tell your body what to do. When you planned the First Kiss, you had to keep telling your lips to relax—right? As your body learns movements, the actions become easy, and you can do them "without thinking," without a conscious act of your will. Just for future reference, keep in mind the idea that your *will* drives *thoughts* into *action*. (See the diagram below.)

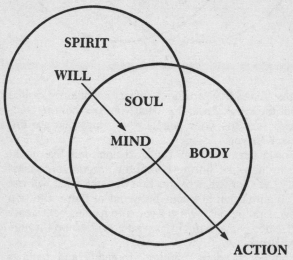

For our purposes there are three levels in the thought patterns zipping or plodding through your mind. Level 1 is what you think and feel—your daily thought processes. Level 2 is attitude—what you like or dislike.

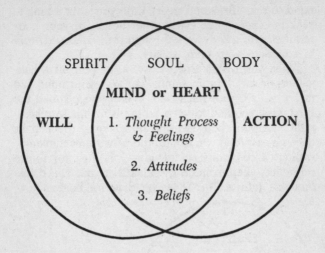

cesses. *Level 2* is attitude—what you like or dislike about the input. *Level 3* is what you rock-bottom commit yourself to—your beliefs, the values that are important to you.

For instance, you can think, "I don't feel like plinking through that boring computer programming class today." If your will activates that thought, what will you do? Right. You'll get your body out of there. But you know skipping class will get you into hassles, so it's easy to decide, "Naw, I might as well go and sleep through it as usual."

You collect daily, random thoughts and feelings about computer programming because you're exposed to input about it: your body is in that class, fumbling with the F1 key, blinking at "700 ON B GOSUB 100, 200: REM COMPUTED GOSUB ON 'B' VARIABLE." Whether you've acted on this input or not, you'll at some point come to Level 2. A thought accompanied by feelings will pop into your mind that you hate or love this stuff. Then your will confirms the thought: "Yeah, computer programming is boring," or "Computer programming is really fun!" You've just decided on an attitude.

If you decide to act out an attitude, the action will have a lot of emotion and willpower behind it. If your will activates an "I hate this!" attitude, you'll probably quit the class and sign up for hemp rope tricks. Attitudes are powerful.

To continue the saga of your Computer Class Life, as you collect more thoughts and feelings about computer programming, you form stronger attitudes that eventually lead your thinking to Level 3: belief. A *belief* combines your daily thought processes with your attitudes. You've done a lot of thinking and you have strong feelings about that thinking. Here again, your will pushes your mind to conclude that what you think and feel is *the way it is*.

Level 3 is what you actually think is true in your own life. Beliefs aren't easily expressed, but if they are, they come out starting with something like "I really think. . . ." You might tell yourself, "I really think computer programming is for eggheads, and I ain't one," or "I really think this is going to be my ticket to success."

Get used to thinking about your thinking—your thoughts, feelings, attitudes, and beliefs. Try making a list of Level 3 beliefs that you uphold. What are the attitudes behind those beliefs?

THE CASE OF THE CHOCOLATE ECLAIR
So, how do all these brain-busting ideas fit together? Let's explore how they work in just one case—that of one hungry writer and an extremely tempting chocolate eclair.

SAGA OF A CHOCOLATE ECLAIR

INTERNAL   **EXTERNAL**

INPUT: the eclair
is sighted

SPIRIT   **SOUL**   **BODY**
will   *mind*   *brain*

**thought
patterns**

ACTION: the eclair
disappears in two
dainty bites

1. My eyes spy the dainty morsels and zap the sensory info to my brain as input: "Chocolate eclairs! Chocolate eclairs!"

2. My mind catches the brain's recognition and fond memories of chocolate eclairs. The discs begin to whir. Attitudes pop up such as "I love 'em!" and "If God didn't want us eating eclairs, He wouldn't have made chocolate in the first place" and "One tiny eclair won't hurt me at all." Some basic beliefs about my nutritional needs, my privilege of enjoying sugar blasts, and my regular calorie-burning exercise chime in.

3. My will—one of the basic ingredients in *me*—activates one of the choices that emerge in the hodge-podge of my thought patterns.

4. My external action (you guessed it) reveals what's gone on internally (see Matthew 7:16-20).

Note that the input started the whole process, but *it* wasn't responsible for the final action, right? *I* was. And I had to make some decisions as acts of my will before I chomped into that eclair. So let's add these concepts to the other points we've hit in this chapter:

▶ Your brain is not the same as your mind.

▶ Your mind is interconnected to both the physical and spiritual dimensions through your spirit and body.

▶ Your will is what activates any thought or feeling, attitude or belief into action.

▶ Chocolate eclairs are not necessarily sinful.

4

Paradise. Imagine it.

Direct your brain as if it were a computer disk and dredge up what's stored on the topic of the Garden of Eden. You'll have impressions of old Sunday School cartoons, probably a few classical paintings, a few details that you've imagined on your own.

What do you see? Chocolate eclairs hanging from the trees? Lush vegetation and sunlight? Adam and Eve with no tan lines? Well, let's stuff some more input into your mind. Maybe you'll discover a few new thoughts, form new attitudes and beliefs about why it's so tough for our supposedly amazing minds to put much amazement into our everyday lives. Something happened back there in Eden that is literally mind-boggling.

FRANKENSTEIN AND HIS BRIDE IN EDEN
Nearly every myth passed from generation to generation in most cultures describe man's beginning in connection with a paradise, sometimes specifically a garden paradise. (Sorry, evolutionists, even mankind's

Forbidden Persimmons

myths and legends don't support the idea that man arose from lower forms of life. The stories nearly always tell of the first man and/or woman descending from a higher being or higher state, not ascending from lower life.)

God created the first man and woman and gave them the gift of rulership over everything:

> Then God said, "Let Us make man in Our image, according to Our likeness; and let them rule over the fish of the sea and over the birds of the sky and over the cattle and over all the earth. . . ." And God blessed them; and God said to them, "Be fruitful and multiply, and fill the earth, and subdue it; and rule" (Genesis 1:26, 28).

Man was created as master of things. Man was the only creation made in God's image, the only "thing" given a spirit to interact with his physical body (Genesis 2:7). Man—with his and her spirit and mind—was designed to control the material world. It was a case of *mind* over *matter*.

Adam and Eve had three distinct advantages in controlling the world.

First, they communed, mind to mind, with the God of the universe. They walked and talked in the garden (Genesis 3:8) and asked Him everything they could think of: "Exactly how did You create this planet? (Genesis 1:1-19); "How can we be male and female and still both be created in Your image?" (Genesis 1:27); "What's the best way to handle these animals, and what're they for?" (Genesis 1:28) Use your imagination; if you'd had endless days of picking the mind of the Source of Wisdom of the universe, what would you ask? Imagine what you could learn! Imagine what they *did* learn.

Second, their minds were uncluttered. Adam and

Eve were completely free of the worries and problems that clutter our minds today. Adam and Eve never had to worry about wearing the "right" clothes, or passing algebra, or getting a date for Saturday night. There were no telephone bills, no mosquito bites, no parents, no nuclear fallout, no TV commercials, no empty wallets, no dentists. In that mysterious area where their perfect bodies and perfect spirits overlapped, Adam and Eve could think without distraction. Their minds could collect and analyze all the input their senses and spirits could provide.

Third, their brains operated at a perfect 100 percent efficiency. When God made Adam and Eve, His creatures were "very good" (Genesis 1:31). And when God makes something that's very good, you better believe it works the way it was supposed to work. The physical brains of the first humans operated perfectly.

When you were conjuring up mental pictures of Eden, did you imagine Adam and Eve as sort of Neanderthals? Or at least as innocent bimbos who stood around munching fruit, waiting for something to happen? Wrong. They weren't anything like the kind of Frankenstein creature man himself would "create." These people chit-chatted with the only infinitely intelligent Being in the universe. They had no worries or distractions, and they operated at peak thoughtpower as masters of God's creation.

PERSIMMONS RUINED EVERYTHING

Then Adam and Eve ate persimmons (Genesis 3). (I'm sure it was persimmons. They're the most forbidding fruit *I* ever bit into.)

By disobeying God, Adam and Eve bit into a whole new program. Their old ways of thinking got the axe because their spirits immediately died (Genesis 2:17). Death in the Bible always suggests a separation. For instance, physical death is separation of the spirit from the body (Matthew 27:50). Adam and Eve died instantly when their spirits were separated from the Spirit of the Life-Giver. Their spirits still existed, just as a dead physical body still exists. But they were now unresponsive to the Spirit of God, as a dead physical body is unresponsive.

Man lost access to the Source of Wisdom. As of that day, his thinking would no longer be God-centered. Immediately the first humans were ashamed to chat about pruning the breadfruit trees with God since there was now disobedience and guilt between them. They lost their walks and talks with God (Genesis 3:8-10). And the broken fellowship was passed to all of us: "Through one man sin entered into the world, and death through sin, and so death spread to all men ... for by the transgression of the one the many died.... Through one transgression there resulted condemnation to all men" (Romans 5:12, 15, 18).

Man's mind was darkened. His thinking would become twisted. Remember the diagram of the soul? How it's the overlapping of the spirit and body? Well, it's not too tough to see why man's deadened spirit began affecting his heart or mind, which is centered in the soul. God's warning about disobedience was literally "you shall surely die" (Genesis 2:17)—suggesting that the immediate death of man's spirit would be accompanied by a gradual death in his whole being.

Generation by generation, man's thinking became progressively warped as spiritual decay set in.

Their *thinking* became futile and their foolish *hearts* were darkened. Although they claimed to be wise, they became fools. . . . Therefore, God gave them over in the sinful desires of their *hearts*. . . . Furthermore, since they did not *think* it worthwhile to retain the knowledge of God, He gave them over to a depraved *mind* (Romans 1:21-28, NIV).

Man's thinking would become so warped that spiritual truth would seem only foolish to him (1 Corinthians 2:14).

Thinking now became controlled by a sin nature ("the flesh" in Colossians 2:18), depraved and deprived of the truth (1 Timothy 6:5), and accompanied by a contaminated conscience (Titus 1:15).

Man's brain began to decay. His thinking would be limited as his dead spirit infected his body. Sin brought death into even the physical realm. Adam and Eve's bodies began to grow old along with all of nature. With dead spirits, darkening minds, and decaying bodies, Adam and Eve didn't have the ability to be masters of creation anymore. Cut off from God, with darkened, limited thinking, man's mind couldn't handle God's level of wisdom (Job 28:12-13; 1 Corinthians 1:19-20). Instead of mind over matter, it became *matter over mind*.

The physical sight of their own bodies forced Adam and Eve to make clothes and to hide in the garden (Genesis 3:7-8). Thorns and thistles began to hassle their efforts at growing food. Physical pain began afflicting the human race (Genesis 3:17-18). Weeds, wrinkles, and work continually reminded Adam and Eve that they'd lost their positions as masters of everything in the world. And all their descendents' thinking processes would now be cut off from the Source of Wisdom, darkened, and limited.

BACK IN THE SADDLE AGAIN
God knew man would want to sneak back into the garden again—where he'd have life easy, where he'd

have mastery over everything again. So God placed an angel with a flaming sword at the gate of Eden (Genesis 3:24) until the garden decayed into dust.

The generations following Adam and Eve no doubt knew what life was like before the Fall. Since the decay of spiritual death took time to creep into man's body, the early humans lived for centuries. Adam died at 930! Seth was 912, Kenan was 910, etc. (See Genesis 5.) Thousands of Adam and Eve's offspring could sit down with the old couple and talk about the old days. Adam and Eve would have shared everything God had told them about the universe.

Since the Apostle Paul suggests that the darkening of man's mind was progressive, the early generations undoubtedly could think through this information better than we can today. In the beginning, Adam and Eve had 100 percent use of their brain power. Most brain experts today suggest we use no more than 10 percent of our brain's abilities. In fact, many scientists agree with brain specialist Peter Russell. "We probably do not use even 1 percent—more likely 0.1 percent or less" (*The Brain Book* by Peter Russell, Hawthorne Books Inc., 1979.)

The mysterious, amazing wonders and legends of the ancient world aren't so surprising when you consider the ancients' contact with the paradise couple, the hundreds of years they had to experiment, the universal language they all shared, and the mental powers of early man. When men organized to build the Tower of Babel so they could get back to paradise, they were so advanced that God said "nothing which they purpose to do will be impossible for them" (Genesis 11:6).

PARADISE FOUND?

Whether it's called Utopia, paradise, or just "the perfect lifestyle," we still feel we've got to get ourselves back to the garden. Most of our antics, dreams, and efforts are just complicated patterns of wishing for the beauty, innocence, and power of paradise. We want to return to "mind over matter." We want to control the temperature in our houses, which radio stations we listen to, the speed of our Subarus, and each other. We think that if we were in control of things, we could make our lives perfect.

Lots of people take the physical road back to paradise. Trying to control physical things like our bodies and our environment is big business; it's called science. The goal of science is to analyze what makes things tick, so we can ultimately control that ticking. We study nature so we can control nature. We break down the properties of geological strata so we can control the geothermal pressures in order to harness power. We study viruses so we can control disease. We experiment with rocket thrusters so we can conquer space. Science and technology want to improve where and how we live so we'll have all the comforts of a physical paradise.

Grooming the body for paradise is also popular. Focus on the body, make it comfortable, give it pleasure, make it healthy and strong, and everything else in life will fall in place. Of course, even an airhead who spends every waking moment pumping iron and guzzling brewers' yeast will admit that life doesn't become perfect with even a perfect combination of rest, exercise, and diet. Killer biceps still can't control everything in life.

The switch of "mind over matter" to "matter over mind" wasn't caused by a physical problem. So it can't be "fixed" physically.

Some people believe the loss of paradise was a mental/ emotional problem. This more sophisticated view suggests that man's vague problem is an inner one, so the focus is on the mind. We can regain paradise through proper education.

If you get the right education, you'll be able to get a wonderful job, which will allow you to control your life. You can buy a car, house, stereo, annual vacations in Budapest, and more anchovy pizza than you can possibly eat. You can surround yourself with comfortable and pleasurable things which you can control. The magazine ads that picture the well-paid young professionals grinning through life suggest that nice things and the prestige that goes with them will slide you right back through the gates, regardless of any flaming-sworded angel.

But education obviously includes more than learning job skills. Perhaps adequate education in philosophy, world literature, psychology, history, etc. will educate us into Utopia and make life perfect again.

Paradise wasn't lost because of ignorance. In "the futility of their mind" (Ephesians 4:17), there are millions of wonderfully educated people who are "always learning and never able to come to the knowledge of the truth" (2 Timothy 3:7). Getting worldly wise, packing in those facts and developing emotional stability is good, but it still won't revive a dead man. And that is the problem, right? Man's spirit is dead.

BEYOND THE MIND

Since Adam and Eve lost paradise because of a spiritual problem, it makes sense to focus on the spirit to patch up the problems and regain paradise, right? You've even got choices in the patching-up process: you can work on your own spirit; you can turn to other spirit beings called angels; or you can turn back to the Spirit of God.

Religiously whipping your own spirit back into paradise-shape is an admirable goal in life, but it's sort of like performing do-it-yourself brain surgery. The Apostle Paul (a guy who did a lot of thinking about thinking) said the self-discipline of subjecting the body to the will is noble but useless: "These are matters which have the appearance of wisdom in self-made religion and self-abasement and severe treatment of the body, but are of no value against fleshly indulgence" (Colossians 2:23).

Spiritually aware people who meditate or chant or study spiritual exercises usually get a deeper sense of what life's about, but they still don't get back into paradise. They'll usually be the first to admit they're still only on the path. Meanwhile, fleas bite even mystics. Lots of fine folks allow angelic spirits to help them toward regaining the control man once had in paradise. The only problem with this approach is that the angelic spirits who respond to people's incantations are the bad angelic spirits. The evil ones. Demons.

Evil spirits usually don't present themselves as anything but good spirits. "Even Satan disguises himself as an angel of light" (2 Corinthians 11:14). Demons are more than happy to give humans tantalizing tastes of what it was like for man's mind to control his body, to control other people as if they're things, and to control matter.

Picture a fire pit which glows and smokes. Images of the bystanders shimmer in the heatwaves. The participants have carefully written on each piece of kindling, "I pray safe and beneficent firewalking." Each firewalker has a three-legged crow design on his bandana and tunic. Each slips the mala—the string of 108 beads plus one skull bead—through his fingers and chants a mantra. Then, in a trance, each stumbles and dances on the redhot coals along a 20 to 30-foot trench of fire. The skin isn't burned. It's another spirit-controlled miracle of mind over matter, of the power of the immaterial over the material body.

With occult and psychic power, these spirits can empower a person's mind to bend and move objects without touching them, to travel outside the body, to read minds, to see visions of the past and future, to heal wounds or cause injury, to avoid or cause pain.

A person sold out to the spirits delights "in self-abasement and the worship of angels, taking his stand on visions he has seen, inflated without cause by his fleshly mind" (Colossians 2:18). The tastes of paradise life provided by evil spirits are temporary and devastating.

Remember the third choice for reviving man's spirit, for getting back to the garden with "mind over matter" and walks and talks with the universe's Source of Truth and Wisdom? Yes, you guessed it, you clever reader, you. The last choice is best. Man's spiritual problem of losing paradise can be regained. His mind can be renewed with truth through the spiritual help of the Spirit of God.

5

When Adam and Eve contaminated themselves and their descendents with sin, God immediately announced the solution. His solution wasn't for them to improve their surroundings, take up aerobics, study linguistics, or meditate on their navels. (Wait a minute; they didn't even *have* navels.) God told Satan, "I will put enmity between you and the woman, and between your seed and her seed; he shall crush you on the head and you shall bruise him on the heel" (Genesis 3:15).

DEATH FROM ADAM; LIFE FROM CHRIST

Nearly every culture in history has some legend or myth about some special one who will someday appear and crush the people's enemies. Usually the coming one is to be miraculously born without a father since he's to be from the "seed" of the woman. All these legends are distortions of the original promise that One would come to save all of mankind by crushing the Enemy.

God provided this 100 percent solution since He

The 100-Percent Solution

knew man couldn't solve the problem himself. Thousands of years after the promise of Genesis 3:15, the "seed of the woman" crushed Satan on a cross: "The free gift is not like the transgression. For if by the transgression of one the many died, much more did the grace of God and the gift by the grace of the one Man Jesus Christ abound to the many. . . . For the wages of sin is death, but the gift of God is eternal life in Christ Jesus our Lord" (Romans 5:15; 6:23). "The first man, Adam, became a living soul" when he was created, but Christ, "the last Adam, became a life-giving spirit" (1 Corinthians 15:45).

When the Apostle Paul complained about how wretched he felt, he pleaded for someone to set him "free from the body of this death" (Romans 7:24). Paul found God's solution. "For the law of the Spirit of life in Christ Jesus has set you free from the law of sin and of death" (Romans 8:2).

Did you think God's solution was different in Adam's day from now? Nope. The solution was stated as input into Adam and Eve's minds. They could think about it, talk it over, figure out what it all could mean. And then, ultimately, they would have to—as an act of their wills—decide whether God's statement was true or not. In order to receive God's gift of new life, they would have to believe what God said about the coming One in the deepest levels of their minds and hearts.

Believing what God has said is called faith. Faith has always been the way man reaches out to receive God's 100 percent solution.

If Adam was saved from the problem of his dead spirit, he was saved by faith. The people of the Old Testament gained approval from God by believing what He'd said (Hebrews 11:2). A lot of Christians seem to think Old Testament saints were saved from spiritual death by keeping the Law or giving sacrifices. But the Law was just a very strict schoolmaster that proved man couldn't solve his problem himself (Galatians 3:11, 24). Old Testament sacrifices were only "a reminder of sins year by year. . . . For it is impossible for the blood of bulls and goats to take away sins" (Hebrews 10:3-4). Salvation was always by believing in what God had promised.

I always think the Before-Christ folks had it tougher than we do today. Imagine how hard it must have been to believe when the One hadn't come yet. Now, Christ's coming is history. Everything is spelled out in black and white.

▶ Nobody's perfect, so we're all cut off from our perfect God. "For all have sinned and fall short of the glory of God" (Romans 3:23).

▶ If something isn't done about the death in our spirit, we'll just keep being spiritually dead, cut off from God. When that goes on day after day, it's called a rotten life. When it goes on after life on earth, it's called Hell. When it goes on forever, it's called the Lake of Fire where we'll remain cut off from the life of God: "For the wages of sin is death" (Romans 6:23).

▶ God provided the 100 percent solution as He promised: "God demonstrates His own love to us, in that while we were yet sinners, Christ died for us" (Romans 5:8). Jesus was separated from the Father on the cross (Matthew 27:46), taking on Himself all the separation and death and Hell we're destined for. He could do it all at once for all of us because He's infinite (Hebrews 9:25-28).

▶ Jesus didn't stay dead; He came alive again. Now, by His Spirit, He can come into your spirit and give you His life: "He who has the Son has the life; he who does not have the Son of God does not have the life" (1 John 5:12).

Now, as in all of history since the day Adam and Eve sinned, each of us has a choice: Do I want to have life in my spirit the way I was designed, and to be rejoined with God? After all, God is God, and He is to be obeyed—as Adam and Eve found out. He has a different way of thinking, and if I adopt His views on things, it'll be a real change of mind for me. I'll have to repent (Acts 2:38)—literally, change my mind—about the thinking that says I can and should run my own life.

Or do I want to exist forever as a dead spirit with a darkened soul and a decayed body? Do I *believe* God's promise and His warnings? I mean the deep-level believing. Do I believe Him enough to activate that belief and tell Him I want Him in my life? "If [I] confess with [my] mouth Jesus as Lord, and believe in [my] heart that God raised Him from the dead, [I] shall be saved" (Romans 10:9). I'll be on my way back to the garden where I commune with the Source of Wisdom (Romans 5:1), where my mind is being renewed to be like it was in the beginning (Ephesians 4:23-24), where I'll get a perfect new body free from sin's effects (1 Corinthians 15:42-49).

It's your choice, right? Your thought processes can mull over this input of God's 100 percent solution. You can decide whether it's true, then your will can choose to activate that belief. If you're not sure you've made your choice yet, do it now. "I call heaven and earth to witness. . . , I have set before you life and death, the blessing and the curse. So choose life in order that you may live . . . for this is your life" (Deuteronomy 30:19-20).

NOT THE SAME OLD SONG AND DANCE

All right. Level with me. What were you thinking about through that section? Here you are, reading this Christian book, thinking, "Doesn't this guy know only Christians would bother reading this? Who else would risk boredom and 'thou shalt' on top of 'thou shalt not' by reading a Christian book?"

Maybe while your eyes read over the words, you buzzed off and started thinking about when you were a little kid and you played chain gang with the neighbors by tying your shoestrings together. Maybe you yawned, "Oh, here's the same old song and dance of get saved and everything's fine." Maybe you skipped it altogether.

I wanted to hit you with that section on what it means to be saved because: (1) about half of the "Christian" youth I meet "asked Jesus into their heart" as toddlers and now aren't sure they're really saved; (2) lots of Christians spout phrases about salvation as if they're born-again parrots, but it seems that few stop at new levels of maturity to think through salvation in new, different, deeper ways; and (3) climbing into a life of dazzling, new thinking demands a clear understanding of how it's all possible.

The key, of course, is making sure that the entrance of Christ's Spirit has made your spirit alive. When you're "born of the Spirit" (John 3:5), you become "a new creature; the old things passed away; behold, new things have come" (2 Corinthians 5:17). One of the new things that has come is your new nature (2 Peter 1:4), a "new self who is being renewed to true knowledge according to the image of the One who created [you]" (Colossians 3:10). Which means that you had an old self, right? Although it's actually impossible to draw a "nature" or a "self," let's try to "diagram" the old you. You do the fill-in part, using diagonal lines to represent the parts of you controlled by sin and its effects.

Remember, your dead spirit contaminated your soul and your body with sin and its effects. Your old self, or old nature, or what the Bible refers to often as "flesh" is the state of sin controlling all of you—body, soul, and spirit. Don't confuse the old nature "flesh" with the body. They're not the same.

How does living in the flesh or old nature affect a

AN OLD-NATURE SELF PORTRAIT

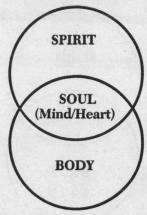

Fill in the parts of you controlled by sin when living in the "flesh."

person's mind? "Those who are according to the flesh set their minds on the things of the flesh . . . for the mind-set of the flesh is death . . . the mind set on the flesh is hostile toward God, for it does not subject itself to the law of God, for it is not even able to do so; and those who are in the flesh cannot please God" (Romans 8:5-8).

If a person belongs to Christ through salvation, he has the Spirit. In fact, "if anyone does not have the Spirit of Christ, he does not belong to Him" (Romans 8:9). Now, diagram on page 56 what happens when the Spirit of God steps into your life. Keep in mind that "if Christ is in you, though the body is dead because of sin, yet the spirit is alive because of righteousness" (Romans 8:10). Put diagonal lines across the part of you still under sin's control at the moment of salvation. Did you have a little trouble deciding what to do

A NEW-NATURE SELF PORTRAIT

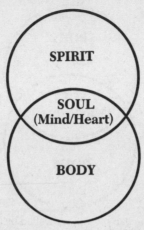

Fill in the parts of you controlled by sin after salvation takes place.

with that middle area—your soul? It's obvious by the zits, crooked teeth, and sore toes of our bodies that they're still contaminated by sin. And the soul's mind is connected to the body through the brain. But the soul is a tricky thing, remember? When the Holy Spirit first steps in and whenever our will chooses, He is in control of not only our *spirits* but our *minds* as well. "Those who are according to the Spirit [set their minds] on the things of the Spirit . . . the mind set on the Spirit is life and peace" (Romans 8:5-6). So your diagram should have had diagonal lines only through the "body" segment.

That pretty well represents the new nature—the "new self, which in the likeness of God has been created in righteousness and holiness of the truth" (Ephesians 4:24).

SIN AIN'T GOT NOTHIN' ON YOU

When you're hoofing through your day choosing to act under the Holy Spirit's control in your spirit, you're living according to your new nature. You're enjoying the all-in-the-family fellowship Adam and Eve lost (Romans 8:15-16) Your mind is being renewed by input from God's Spirit (Romans 12:2 and Colossians 3:10) and your heart is emotionally burned by these new thoughts (Luke 24:32). You should know that the effects of imperfection on your body are only temporary, since "if the Spirit of Him who raised Jesus from the dead dwells in you, He who raised Christ Jesus from the dead will also give life to your mortal bodies through His Spirit who indwells you" (Romans 8:11; see also 8:23 and 1 Corinthians 15:20-22, 35-54).

Stick with me. This is probably the least-discussed and most critical stuff you can think through.

What happened to your old self, your old nature? "Our old self was crucified with Him, that our body of sin might be done away with, that we should no longer be slaves to sin" (Romans 6:6). Has the old self disappeared in a poof of spiritual enthusiasm? Nope. When you're in your new nature, you're just dead (unresponsive) to the old self—cut off from it. Paul writes, "Therefore do not let sin reign in your mortal body that you should obey its lusts, and do not go on presenting the members of your body to sin as instruments of unrighteousness. . . . For sin shall not be master over you" (Romans 6:12-14).

A Christian doesn't *have* to step out of his new nature. Let's make this personal. I sin because as an act of my will I decide to. You sin because you decide to. As with everything else that goes on inside the real you, giving in to the old sin nature is an act of your will.

There are a lot of old-self memories, old-nature attitudes, and old-self beliefs recorded in that amazing brain of yours, so it's easy to give in to the old ways of

PORTRAIT OF A SAVED PERSON
LIVING IN THE FLESH

Fill in a diagram of a saved person who is living under his old nature.

handling situations, acting in the old-self ways. But get responsible. Think it through until you really believe that *you choose to let the Holy Spirit control your life from your spirit or to let sin control your life from your body (Romans 6:13, 16).*

Remembering that Christ by His Spirit promised never to leave us (Hebrews 13:5), fill in a quick diagram of a saved person who has decided to live according to the old self.

When you're living according to your old self, the power of sin controls your mind. You've lost the walk-and-talk fellowship you enjoyed with God. Your mind isn't being renewed. Your body with its old-nature-stuffed brain seems to dictate your life. A Christian living according to the flesh feels just like, thinks just like, and seems just like a non-born-again natural child of Adam and Eve.

As you're reading this right now, you may be reading according to your old sin nature. You find yourself feeling the same old attitudes, and thinking the same old thoughts. I don't know how many Sunday School lessons I sat through with my mind controlled by my old self. As a matter of fact, I don't know how many Sunday School lessons I've *taught* when my thinking was darkened and limited, when my heart was hardened because I was operating under my old self.

But we're new creations in Christ, remember? Old things are passed away (2 Corinthians 5:17). Even though I sometimes let sin kick my body and mind around, I've been "sealed in Him with the Holy Spirit of promise" (Ephesians 1:13). With the solid presence of God's Spirit in me, I can always choose to say no to sin and yes to Him.

FILLED WITH THE SPIRIT FOR A THINK TANK FILL-UP

"If we confess our sins, He is faithful and righteous to forgive us our sins, and to cleanse us from all unrighteousness" (1 John 1:9) wouldn't be in the Bible if God didn't expect us to sin. It's a classic verse. For those of us with bizarre wills, it's a life-saver. Memorize it. Use it. Now.

Really. Ask God right now if there's anything that you need to confess. The Holy Spirit will quickly convict you of anything you need to talk over (John 16:8). Now confess whatever comes to mind.

Confession isn't begging for forgiveness or foaming at the mouth in passion. A criminal's confession to the police isn't "Please, guys, forgive me; I'm so miserably sorry; etc." Confession is literally "saying the same words" God would say about what you've done, having the same attitude He does about it.

When He then forgives and cleanses you from all

unrighteousness, He really forgives you and cleanses you from *all* unrighteousness. And you're right back under the Holy Spirit's control, when the direction for your life comes from God's spiritual dimension (mind over matter). Your mind is ready to be renewed and reprogram your brain according to the "Spirit of truth" (John 14:17).

Instead of being controlled by physical things like mosquito itches, racy hormones, peer pressure, or wine, you're now controlled by the Spirit. This is exactly the sense of the phrase "be filled with the Spirit" (Ephesians 5:18). Being *filled* with the Spirit is being *controlled* by the Spirit. Being filled by the Spirit step by step is called "walking in the Spirit." "If we live by the Spirit, let us also walk by the Spirit." (Galatians 5:25 makes good sense to me.)

Why did we plow through such a heavy Bible study about the role of the Holy Spirit in our lives? First, because our realignment with the God of the universe—being saved and controlled by Him—is the most important thing we can ever understand. And I wanted to be sure you were with me on those killer concepts. Second, when it comes to thinking about thinking, the Holy Spirit's role is absolutely, positively indispensable. It's not me, it's not you, and it's obviously not any of your teachers, but it *is* the "Spirit of truth [who] will guide you into all the truth" (John 16:13). And His guidance into truth starts by helping you think about the first phase of thinking: input.

6

Remember the basic layout of thinking?

INPUT ◊ THOUGHT PATTERNS ◊ LIFE PATTERNS

Your *life pattern*—your outward behavior—is pretty obvious stuff. You relace your basketball shoes with pink flourescent laces, you try a suck on a marijuana cigarette, you kiss a frog, you swear under your breath, you end a prayer with "please," you spray shaving cream into Terry McCormack's locker, etc.

The *thought patterns* of your brain, mind, and heart are not so obvious. But we've at least sketched how your actions are a result of beliefs, attitudes, or thoughts and feelings activated by your will.

Input seems like the simplest factor in all this thinking business, and yet it too is a complex topic.

100,000 BITS A SECOND
How many distinct chunks of input are hitting your mind right now? Scientists say thousands of bits of

Input that Doesn't Quit

information can be processed in your brain each second—information about everything from each of the letters making up these words to the amount of light that's on the book, to how your hands feel holding it, to the uncomfortable ache in your leg, to what Cheryl said to you yesterday, to the music in the background, to. . . . Fortunately, your brain ignores most of the input pouring in, because trying to think about each bit of input would give you a brain-chatter headache for life!

Where does input come from? Instinct or heredity provides the most basic input for your thinking. Information planted genetically in the brains of both humans and animals provides food for thought. For instance, Paul tells us the thought that God exists is instinctive in every human, regardless of culture, environment, or upbringing. *Maybe a God exists* will cross every human's mind at some point in his life "because that which is known about God is evident within them; for God made it evident to them" (Romans 1:19).

Images and information from the spiritual dimension also enter your mind as input. God's Spirit (see 1 John 2:27) and Satan himself (see John 13:2) can introduce thoughts into the human mind.

Your physical state can affect your thinking. For instance, an underactive thyroid gland can cause you to think more slowly than normal. Drugs, injury, illness, physical stress, lack of sleep, shock therapy, etc. can pop thoughts into your mind.

Your senses, of course, are the main sources of the input that clambers through your brain into your heart/mind. Your abilities to see, hear, physically feel, smell, and taste provide an incredible number of tidbits for thought.

Input also comes from your memory—from your brain's recorded thoughts, impressions, images, and conclusions.

Often your mind struggles to put together input from *all* these sources. Try to imagine the input Annie Brotherton's mind tied together the night she yawned and said, "I'm sure glad they can't kill stars." All these sources of input contribute to the brain chatter rattling through your head—input produced by God (as in Acts 8:29), by others (not just friends and family, but stereo, radio and TV, as well), and by yourself. You're drenched with input. That makes it a bit dangerous.

INPUT OVERLOAD

The sheer mass of input that clobbers your mind makes it a little dangerous because you might get tired and simply accept it all as true. As a Spirit-controlled Christian, you can be exposed to all kinds of ideas, statements, perceptions, and images. You can think about each thing, weigh it for truth or error, and tuck your Spirit-guided conclusion about it into your mind. But when you are overwhelmed with too much input to think about, how can you reach solid conclusions?

I just got back from a smoked-turkey-and-cheddar-cheese-sandwich-break at the Ozark Smokehouse. After I'd wolfed down platefuls of goodies, I sat back and thought about this input stuff. "Anything else?" the waitress asked. Ten minutes later she asked twice, "Are you sure you don't want anything else?"

"No thanks, just thinking," I said.

"Problems?"

"No, just thinking about thinking," I said.

She raised her eyebrows as if I still had mayonnaise on my mustache. "That's odd," she said. "Odd."

I guess it is. If it's not thinking about problems, thinking as a pastime *is* a little odd these days. Ever craved some tranquil time to just sit and think about it all? The modern person's daily schedule doesn't allow for hours of thinking time, yet there are thousands of input-tidbits we *need* to think about every day.

So let me offer two shreds of advice. First, if you've never really thought through the input you've been exposed to so far in life—if you're not sure what you really believe—don't go looking desperately for more exciting, controversial input.

For example, if you don't really understand how the Spirit guides you, you're nuts to tackle a study of the occult. If you don't know about the reasons behind God's commands about sex, you're a mental if you think you can wisely handle the sensual input of a sexual experience. If you're an alcoholic who doesn't understand why booze gets a hold on you, you're an airhead if you think you can wisely process the input— the smells, sights, and sounds—of a beer bust.

Second, if you don't spend much time seriously thinking about what you're reading, watching, hearing, and feeling, be assured that while some of the input is true, a lot of it is 100 percent baloney. So don't just suck it all in.

Be careful of the barrage of input swirling around you. Unthinking acceptance of all input is dangerous. You might start thinking false input is true, or you might start forming attitudes and beliefs that you've never really thought through.

TRUE OR FALSE, GOOD OR EVIL?

Input can be true (God exists; I just ate a smoked turkey sandwich; you are reading these words; etc.) or false (Sex is dirty; God needs your offering money; I'm writing this from Tahiti; etc.). But one of the most difficult things to accept about input is that it is neither good nor bad.

If that stumps you, think through the fact that although the statement "Sex is dirty" is false, the letters and words themselves aren't evil. Although my toes are sending my brain *true* messages of "We're cold," those messages don't have anything to do with "goodness" or "godliness."

Words, images, and sensory input are neither godly nor sinful. Paul tells us, "I know and am convinced in the Lord Jesus that nothing is unclean in itself; but to him who thinks anything to be unclean, to him it is unclean" (Romans 14:14). "To the pure, all things are pure" (Titus 1:15).

What the mind *does* with input is what's good or bad, godly or sinful. The worst profanity listed in a dictionary of slang is morally neutral until its input reaches a human mind and that mind "acts" on the input.

It's dangerous to disbelieve Paul's teaching. You might convince yourself that if you're surrounded by what's labeled "good" input, you'll be good. (Ask any kid in any Christian school in the world if a "Christian atmosphere" keeps kids who want to sin from sinning like Pancho Villa.) And you might convince yourself that if you're surrounded by "evil input," you'll have no choice but to be contaminated.

Input itself is neutral. What you *do* with input becomes good or evil. So *you*—not the input hitting you—are responsible for the godliness or sinfulness in your life. Don't count on what's labeled "good" input to make you good, and don't blame "evil" input for your evil. ("I can't act like a Christian around those guys," "He just kept pressuring me until I had to give in and sleep with him," "Everybody was drinking and I couldn't resist," etc.)

Because input is neutral, you can accept useful input generated by even unpleasant, false, or sinful people. For instance, even though Benjamin Franklin fathered several illegitimate children, his advice that "A stitch in time saves nine" is good food for thought! Under the Spirit's guidance, studying the "God is dead" point of view can provide interesting, useful information on how some people think. Listening to the ideas of a non-Christian athlete is vital to reaching non-Christian athletes for Christ.

Jesus himself knew that the contamination of sin comes from what a person does with input, not with the input itself: "Listen to Me, all of you, and understand; there is nothing outside the man which going into him can defile him; but the things which proceed out of the man are what defile the man" (Mark 7:14-15).

Jesus wasn't afraid of input—even if it came from taxgatherers, prostitutes, and known sinners. (See John 17:15 and 1 Corinthians 5:9-10.)

A THREE-MINUTE BIBLE STUDY

First, look up Titus 2:14. (This isn't going to work unless you actually look it up; so look it up.) Notice the phrase "for His own possession" in the *New American Standard Version* and "peculiar" in the *King James Version*. These words are translations of a Greek form of "to be" and the prefix *peri*—meaning "around" as in "*peri*meter" or "*peri*scope." So picture yourself—one of God's people—as a dot and God as a circle "being around" you. Picture a temptation or any tidbit of input as an arrow. Now, what has to happen for that arrow to *hit* you?

Now look up 1 Corinthians 10:13. Will God allow anything in that He knows your will can't handle?

Finally, read James 1:13-16. Think slowly through the progression. The "each one" or "he" is the will. "Lust" is any strong desire. "Enticed" is the action of dangling bait before a fish; input or the temptation itself is the "bait" being held by lust. At what stage does sin appear?

Let's illustrate what you've studied. You're sauntering down your favorite alley, and you step across a gross porno magazine somebody threw out. It's open to an article with a racy photo on one page and the title "A Night in Paradise" on the other. The sight of the thing is the input—the enticement or bait. (Have you sinned yet?)

What happens next? Your natural, strong desire for sexual experience says, "This could be extremely interesting," dangling the input in front of your will. (Have you sinned yet?)

Then you make a decision. It might be to say no to your strong desire, and keep strutting down the alley. (Did you sin by seeing the input?) Or you might decide to give in to your desire, and pick up the magazine and begin mentally using others for your sexual pleasure—which is sin (Matthew 5:28; 1 Corinthians 6:18).

Now, pornography is sick stuff, but who or what is responsible for the sin that circles in your imagination when you pick up and digest a porno article? The models? The photographer or writer? The publisher? The store that sold the thing? The person who bought it and tossed it in the alley? Your parents for letting you walk down that alley? The sickie article itself? Or *you*?

Input is only bait. It doesn't *make* you sin.

Why am I pushing this input-is-neutral idea? Three reasons: (1) it emphasizes your responsibility for what you *do* with input, (2) it lets you consider input from all kinds of sources, and (3) it'll help free you from . . . (step back, folks) . . . Input Phobia!

INPUT PHOBIA

I'm going to stop writing this book for a minute and just talk with you, OK? It'll be kind of an off-the-record conversation about input warnings. Just between me and you—no parents around, no Sunday School teachers.

"Here you go," you say, with a roll of one eye.

"You're going to start trying to make me feel guilty for listening to sinful music and reading sophisticated books and going to movies and watching humanistic TV shows and reading articles about sex and. . . ."

Nope.

"What? Isn't that your whole point for a book on thinking? That we should clean up our nasty young minds?"

Good grief! Relax your defenses for just a minute and let me explain something. Lots of adults—whether parents, youth leaders, ministers, teachers, or whoever—are really concerned about the input that's hitting you youthy types. Well, I guess "concerned" is a flimsy term for it. They're scared.

"Why?"

You know. Because they think that what goes into your head is what comes out in your life. They're afraid that if you see garbage on TV, hear garbage vocabulary at school, and watch garbage violence in a movie, you'll be nothing but garbage yourself.

"Isn't that what you've been saying?"

Nope. Remember, our basic premise is that your life will be the way you think in your heart. Thinking in your heart is the thought pattern phase of our study. Input is just what goes in.

"You mean, Stearns, that what goes into my mind isn't what comes out? Are you getting a little heretical?"

No, but that's why I wanted to talk with just you, since lots of good Christians believe *input* gets kids drunk and sexually involved and on dope and away from the Lord, not the kids themselves. Listen, I don't know how many times I've heard motivating Christian speakers compare my mind to a computer. With computers it's GIGO—Garbage In, Garbage Out, right? But I'm no computer. Thank God, I can choose to decide whether something's true or not. I can choose to accept a viewpoint or believe something.

For instance, I've been saturated for years with how awesomely sophisticated it is to puff on cigarettes. Even as we speak, cigarette manufacturers are spending megabucks on every living man, woman, and child to convince everybody that smoking is impressive, mature, exotic, and attractive. For years jingles, billboard slogans, TV, and magazine shots of macho guys and pretty young things puffing away have poured messages about smoking into my head. And what do I do? Nothing. I don't smoke; never have, and never will.

Garbage in doesn't equal garbage out because I choose to say, "Excuse me? Yellow stains on my teeth and fingers, extra wrinkles, lung cancer, extensive bad breath, the expense of the habit, and ashes all over everything? Cigarettes aren't going to be part of me." In the face of a tremendous amount of input about smoking, I can choose to say *no*.

So now you know. I don't believe in GIGO when it comes to humans. In fact, it seems to me that GIGO advocates are a lot like evolutionists who consider us to be only machines or animals with computer-brains. Monistic thinkers and GIGOists alike seem to believe:

INPUT ◊ LIFE PATTERNS

By the way, did I ever tell you some of my old Army stories or when I worked as a roughneck on offshore oil rigs?

"No," you yawn. "And I can hardly contain my excitement at the idea of hearing some old Army stories and—."

Okay, okay. The point is that I was saturated 24 hours a day with the worst language and behavior I've ever been around. And what scared me was whether my will was strong enough to stamp "This Isn't Going to Be Part of Me" across that kind of input. Hearing swear words won't make you swear; but deciding to swear will.

"Right. *So*?" you say.

So be gracious and mature when you run into adults who are afraid of input and want to keep you from it. They want to protect you. Because they think that if you encounter evil input, you'll automatically do evil as if you don't have a choice. And they hope that if you receive mostly good input, you'll have no choice but to become godly.

Floor them with an answer like, "Thanks for your concern about what my mind is exposed to, but personally, I'm a lot more concerned with strengthening my will, since *that's* what decides what I'll do with the input. That's where I can use some help."

Anyway, thanks for this confidential conversation. I knew you'd understand, but I wasn't so sure about some older types. It's easy in this world for adults to get scared for their kids. I've got four of them, so I know. We start trying to protect kids instead of equip them. We're afraid that you'll believe some ungodly ideas that you run across in your reading, or that you'll be exposed to temptations that are too much for you to handle—even though God promises that's not possible.

It's incredibly hard for parents to trust the Holy Spirit in kids. Why? Partly because we have trouble trusting God to protect you, and partly because of threats like brainwashing, subliminal seduction and mind control.

INPUT PHOBIA MYTHS
Brainwashing doesn't work. Exquisite torture machines, electroshock therapy, mind-altering drugs,

hypnosis, and sensory deprivation techniques were used in the U.S. Central Intelligence Agency's alarming brainwashing program, MKULTRA, in the 1950s. The result? The CIA's mind control technology succeeded in distorting and sometimes destroying the mind's normal function, but failed completely at manipulating the behavior of unwilling victims.

Philip Zimbardo, professor of psychology at Stanford University, said in a recent article on mind control that force, drugs, or other delightful techniques can change behavior, but can't alter beliefs without the cooperation of the victim. Zimbardo concludes, "The available technologies are unable to induce changes in what a person thinks or does," (*USA Today*, Nov. 1980).

"Brainwashing" is a myth of spy and science fiction novels. No one can make you think the way they want you to without your permission.

Subliminal manipulation is feared by many to be a technique that can make you do or think what you don't want to. "Subliminal" means "below threshold," and the idea is to send messages to your eyes or ears at a subconscious level. The mania hit in September 1957 when a public relations executive announced he had projected "Drink Coke" and "Eat Popcorn" on a movie screen at such a low light level that the audience wasn't consciously aware of the messages. Supposedly, Coke and popcorn sales soared, although the executive never produced any evidence to support his claim.

The point about subliminal input is this: Don't be afraid of it. It's just like any other input—such as the person next to you in science whispering, "Hey, jump up and sing 'Smokin' in the Boys' Room.' " Even subliminal input can't bypass your will to make you do something you don't want to do in the first place. It must be considered by your *mind* and activated by your *will* to become an attitude, belief, or action.

Mind control is a semi-myth. In the early '80s, a

religious fanatic named Jim Jones exerted so much control over his followers' minds that 912 of them committed suicide at his command. Nazi war criminals who demonically killed millions of Jews during World War II proved Hitler's expertise in mind control technique. Their defense was that they were simply "following orders." Two Florida teenagers watched a TV movie in which sleeping street bums were set afire, and they then went out to insanely act out the atrocity. Thinking can be influenced.

Does mind control work? Not really. No one can completely control a person's mind as if he's a mindless robot. But that person can be influenced by tempting input. For example, cult members submit to the thinking of the group because that choice satisfies their strong desire for security, acceptance, and prestige they want.

Here's the point: Nobody can make you think anything. You always have a choice to accept input or reject input. No brainwashing, no subliminal messages, no spiritual input from Satan or God Himself can *force* you to think or do anything unless you *choose* to. The choice may be tough. ("Deny your country and we'll call out for pizza. Refuse and we'll tear out your fingernails!") But all these input-producers can do is *influence your choice of what you'll accept or reject.*

With the incredible barrage of input hitting you, with all the disorienting, confusing, stress-producing, humiliating experiences you go through in your social group, with all the smiling offers of acceptance and security you get daily, is anybody trying to influence your thinking?

Do your gym socks stink?

7

Can your thinking be influenced? of course! Otherwise I wouldn't bother writing this book to you. Your thinking can be influenced with:

▶ *truth* (God is love, even when it doesn't seem true.)

▶ *nonessentials* (I'll now control your mind to think of a chilly chocolate milkshake being poured over your head. Did it work?)

▶ *false information* (You've got to look out for #1 since nobody else is looking out for you.)

I come from a family of nine. As I grew up each of us kids thought it was great fun to tell whoppers to the younger ones. "Yes, at midnight a green, oozy monster slides out of your bedroom closet." "Yes, it's true you were adopted." "No, when we move to California we're not going to take you with us."

Children often swallow—hook, line, and sinker—things that aren't true, from tales of Santa Claus to threats that telling lies makes your nose grow. But when you grow up, you can't afford to believe myths and baloney, since you become the way you think.

Brainwarp

The Apostle Paul said, "When I was a child, I used to speak as a child, think as a child, reason as a child; but when I became [an adult] I did away with childish things" (1 Corinthians 13:11). It's time to get very adult about the challenge of evaluating the input we think about, since a lot of it is infernal baloney right out of the pit.

TALES FROM THE OLD DRAGON

Paul warns you to be careful about your thinking, in case "as the serpent deceived Eve by his craftiness, your minds should be led astray from the simplicity and purity of devotion to Christ" (2 Corinthians 11:3). The very names of "the great dragon" suggest deception: he's "the serpent of old who is called the devil ["the accuser"] and Satan ["the adversary"], who deceives the whole world" (Revelation 12:9). How does he do it?

Satan tempts us to deny the truth. From the beginning, Satan lied about what God had said. He told Eve, "You surely shall not die" (Genesis 3:4), adding to the lie an enticement of "you will be like God" (Genesis 3:5).

Satan knows that if he can falsify our basic beliefs about what God has said, our souls with their darkness and bodies with their strong desires will cooperate to keep us in sin, separated from God. So:

►He schemes (Ephesians 6:11).

►He sets enticing snares with bait (such as money) to coax us to deny what God has said (1 Timothy 6:9).

►He's on the prowl like a roaring lion to devour us—to let us destroy our own lives if we believe his lies (1 Peter 5:8).

Satan's schemes work. In fact, they've worked so well for thousands of years that he's succeeded in a general mass mind-control experiment. His lies have darkened the minds of humans so much that he's actually "blinded the minds of the unbelieving" (2 Corinthians 4:4). Satan deceives people into thinking that they're doing their own thing when the truth is that they're doing the will of the devil!

Christians are to "with gentleness correct those who are in opposition, if perhaps God may grant them repentance leading to the knowledge of the truth, and they may come to their senses and escape from the snare of the devil, having been held captive by him to do his will" (2 Timothy 2:25-26).

Satan has even organized a mob to help in his campaign. He's recruited regiments of spirit-being henchmen to help distort God's truths. These demons are actually arranged into ranks: "For our struggle is not against flesh and blood, but against the rulers, against the powers, against the world forces of this darkness, against the spiritual forces of wickedness in the heavenly places" (Ephesians 6:12).

The influence of this diabolical organization is called the "world system" or just "the world" in English translations of the Greek *kosmos*. The many meanings of the word *world* require a pretty hefty word study—which you might browse through in my book *If The World Fits, You're The Wrong Size* (Victor Books). For now, we'll define the world system as an anti-God organization of spirit beings centered around the "evil one" (1 John 5:19).

As spirits, Satan and his henchmen have access to every human being. That means you—whether you're at a wild party or a church youth retreat. "All that is in the world, the lust of the flesh [strong physical desires] and the lust of the eyes [wanting to have what you see] and the boastful pride of life [the be-your-own-god syndrome]" (1 John 2:16), can be used as enticements to lure us away from God's truth.

BLIND LEADERS OF THE BLIND

The world system has fooled people so thoroughly that they spread false messages as enthusiastically as the Deceiver himself. Even the Apostle Peter fell into this trap (see Matthew 16:23.).

It's important to realize that the "world" we're warned about is not "out there" beyond the walls of the church. The world system is not flesh-and-blood people but an invisible system that controls people to do Satan's will. People's devotion to Satan's deception is nearly unbelievable at times. Even before the flood, "every intent of the thoughts of [man's] heart was only evil continuously" (Genesis 6:5), and today, "evil men and [religious] imposters will proceed from bad to worse, deceiving and being deceived" (2 Timothy 3:13).

When people give in to the controlling deception of the world system, you can be sure that lies about God's basic truths will rule their thinking. You can expect distortions of the truth to come from the world's mass communications and educational systems, from world-class authorities, and even from your friends.

The mass communications media of our society revel in baloney. Do a little fact-finding sometime. Set aside about 15 minutes and flip throgh all the TV channels you've got, jotting down all the messages you hear and see that you know are false. The message may be as obvious as "The good guy always wins and never dies" or "If you buy this car, sexy people will want you." Or it may be as subtle as "Sophisticated people drink" or "Sex is the natural first step in a relationship." Do the same with the radio, changing to a new station each time you note a false message—from "The Lord *needs* your contribution to this miraculous work we're doing in Bunga-Bunga Land" to "Oooh, ooh, oooooh, it can't be wrong if it feels so good."

Decide on a lazy Saturday that you'll try to keep

track of how many different media have access to your mind. Notice how often you encounter messages from TV, radio, magazines, records and tapes, billboards, books, newspapers, posters, movies, etc. Which communication medium has the strongest impact on you? Why?

Of course, there's some good mixed in with the fluff. When the media try to inform us through editorials, news reports, documentaries, or stories that dramatize real issues, we're often faced with important truths to consider. At the same time, these informative programs are often produced by limited, darkened thinking that's been influenced by the world system.

Be careful to realize that the hardline news as well as the wimpy fluff of mass communications is thoroughly laced with baloney. You can't be passive and just swallow everything as if it doesn't matter at all.

Remember that—for you—the strongest enticements will accompany the false messages of the medium that has the strongest impact on you. For instance, if top-40 music on the radio is your favorite form of media input, you need to be extra careful to evaluate its messages ("Sex is love," "Pleasure is primo," etc.).

Leaders living by the world's system can deceive with half-baked truths.

Educational authorities appear to be the real thinkers of our age, but if an educator refuses to acknowledge that the spiritual dimension exists, his teaching will give only a limited, darkened view of reality (see 1 Corinthians 1:18-31).

Today's leading thinkers are sometimes outdone in deception by religious leaders—who are, to me, the *real* wolves in sheeps' clothing. Late last night I chanced on a televised preaching service where the speaker casually tossed out tidbit after tidbit of truths straight from the Book. His followers clapped at each of his witticisms, and he seemed to enjoy a wide following in the television audience since his phone lines were constantly active during the meeting. But after about 40 minutes of basically sound biblical teaching, he pulled out his cigar, sat back, and began mumbling about how a thinking Christian has no choice but to believe in three gods (Gods?) instead of the Trinity.

Religious leaders are usually respected as truth-tellers. Yet the New Testament is filled with important warnings about the dangers of false religious teachers who "walk in craftiness, adulterating [watering down] the Word of God" (2 Corinthians 4:2). God and Satan both know how influential false religious leaders are, and yet many Christians seem to think that as long as the guy or lady has a Bible under one arm, he or she must be preaching truth.

Notice the warnings about false teachers, false prophets and false Christians in Matthew 24:24; 2 Corinthians 11:13, 26; 2 Peter 2:1; 1 John 2:26, 4:1. Since Satan can transform himself into an angel of light, expect the same from Satanic religious leaders. They "disguise themselves as servants of righteousness" (2 Corinthians 11:13-15) to try to lead believers away from truth (Matthew 24:24).

False religionists are often popular, since they usually tell people what they want to hear. Paul warns, "For the time will come when they will not endure sound doctrine; but wanting to have their ears tickled, they will accumulate for themselves teachers in accordance to their own desires; and will turn away their ears from the truth, and will turn aside to myths" (2 Timothy 4:3-4; see also 2 Thessalonians 2:1-12).

Even the best biblically sound preacher who slides into his old nature will begin to sprinkle baloney in with the truths of his message. Every authority—whether educational, religious, civil, political, or military—is open to world-system manipulation as he or she gives in to the lust of the flesh, the lust of the eyes, or the boastful pride of life. So the truth about authority figures is: Obey them (Romans 13:1, Ephesians 6:1), but don't accept all their opinions, attitudes, and values as 100 percent pure truth.

Our friends can deceive us, whether they mean to or not. I'll spare you the sermon on the dangers of peer pressure if you'll just try this little exercise:

1. List your three closest friends or acquaintances.
2. After each name, list at least two things that person thinks which you know aren't true.

Peer pressure sometimes hits you in the form of majority opinion. If most people believe something, it must be true. This is the TMFCBW theory: When deciding whether a maggot-infested steak is edible or not, Ten Million Flies Can't Be Wrong. You get the idea. At some time in history, the masses believed the world was flat, a human couldn't live traveling more that 45 m.p.h., bloodsucking leeches could heal diseases, and women couldn't be educated. The majority can be deceptively wrong.

The point about deception is not "Get cynical and suspect everybody!" It's more "Don't believe everything people tell you." In fact, don't believe everything you tell yourself!

SELF-DECEPTION

We can deceive our own hearts (Galatians 6:3, James 1:26).

I'm pretty good at it. I tend to think that what I perceive is what's real, and I usually barge ahead and act on what I think is true. Such as the time I climbed through old lawnmowers, baby cribs, walnut headboards, bashed-up televisions, and car parts at what I thought was a yard sale. "Ain't no yard sale," said the shotgun-toting old man who came out of the house.

"Just a yard. Now git outa here!"

Look back at the chapter two exercise on page 19. Do you still have trouble telling your eyes they're seeing circles instead of spirals? An experiment with children from different economic backgrounds reported that poor kids, when guessing the exact measurements of coins, "saw" quarters as up to 50 percent larger than they really are. Some of the stars you saw in the sky last night don't even exist anymore. The light you saw left their surfaces years ago, and in the meantime they might have completely burned out. Our senses can deceive us into believing that the sun rotates around the earth, that physical pleasure is always a good thing, or that God doesn't exist. Your own senses can deceive you.

Your emotions can deceive you, too. I skulked around the campus of Biola University for weeks once when I owed buddy Bill Mullins some money I had promised to repay quickly. I thought our friendship was over. I thought he hated me. I thought I'd lost what integrity I'd ever had in his eyes. I thought he was panicking about his money. Mullins finally spied me one Thursday morning crawling away under the cafeteria tables. "Where you been?" he stormed. "I haven't seen you for weeks!"

"Uh, I'm sorry about the bucks, I. . . ."

"Huh?" He held me up by the scruff of my neck. "What're you talkin' about?" In reality, Mullins had forgotten about loaning me the money and wasn't worried in the least about it. In my mind, it had been a different story.

Feel familiar? When was the last time you strongly felt one thing only to find out that the truth was exactly the opposite? Your feelings can deceive you into thinking that God hates you, that infatuation is love, or that you're destined to be a loser or nobody cares.

Old-nature thoughts, attitudes, and beliefs contribute to further mindwarp. The false input sucked in during those times you're under old sin-nature power are recorded in your brain. Unless rethought with renewed thinking, they can affect your growth in truth.

For instance, maybe you decided years ago that God isn't really interested in doing anything remarkable in your life. That thought deceives you into doubting that He "is able to do exceeding abundantly beyond all that we ask or think" (Ephesians 3:20).

Self-deception is one of the basic mind-warping effects of drugs, booze, or anything else that forces you to lose your Spirit-control. A couple of nights ago I was out running when I came across a knock-down-drag-out melee of drunks who came bursting out of a bar. One guy kept screaming that this was no way to treat a Viet Nam vet as he attacked the others, yelling that they'd stolen his motorcycle from the front sidewalk. The cops arrived and broke up the fight. In the flashing blue lights I heard them tell the vet that his bike was safe and sound on the *back* sidewalk—right where he'd parked it.

Anything that controls your mind throws the guard of your heart and mind wide open to delusion. For instance, David Wilkerson of *The Cross and the Switchblade* fame said that every Satanized kid he's ever run into got started on drugs.

So beware, beware, okay? Deceiving, distorting truths, adding juicy enticements to false messages is popular practice these days.

HOW TO AVOID INPUT PHOBIA

With all the deception rampant, is it any wonder why Christian adults often resort to restricting input or to encouraging us not to think for ourselves at all?

But the answer isn't to pretend we can stop world-system input, because like it or not we're up to our necks as people who are in the world system (John 17:15, 18). And of course we don't have to stop thinking, since the Holy Spirit will guide us into all truth, cleansing our thinking through the truth of the Word (John 15:3). How do we handle world-class deception?

▶ *Guard your mind and heart* (Proverbs 4:23). Don't even think about passively agreeing with everything and everybody—even authorities and friends. Resist Satan (Ephesians 4:27, James 4:7). Put on the whole armor of God against his world-system schemes (Ephesians 6:11-17).

▶ *Evaluate input*; it's either truth or baloney. Remember there are often mixtures. A friend's gossip might be half-true, a teacher's statements about evolution might contain some facts and some unfounded opinions, an idea about God might sound familiar but be right out of the pit.

▶ *Reject baloney*. With all the deceptive error zeroing in on you, get very good at pronouncing, "That's not true, and it's not going to be part of my life." Set your mind on the truth for a renewed mind.

How do I determine what's gossip or fact or truth or baloney? Glad you asked. Just turn the page.

8

A while back I asked the youth of a church in Aurora, Indiana to list some popular ideas that are actually false. These are a few of the untrue truths they came up with:

▶ They say you're tough and adult if you smoke.
▶ They say we came from apes.
▶ They say blondes have more fun.
▶ They say you might as well cheat because everybody else does.
▶ They say nice guys finish last.
▶ The say the first kiss is the best.

Baloney is a hot-selling item these days; it's cheap. So with all the deceptive input that hits you, it's hard to know what to think, to know what's true and what isn't. For example, see how you do on this True-or-Baloney test. Mark "T" for true and "F" for baloney:

THE TRUE-OR-BALONEY TEST

____ 1. When true love hits, you'll know it.
____ 2. It was young George Washington who said,

Truth Exists: Only Lies Are Invented

"I cannot tell a lie; I chopped down that cherry tree."

____ 3. Life is better to a good person than to an evil, wicked, mean, and nasty one.

____ 4. Sex is best when you're young.

____ 5. God is masculine.

____ 6. There is no life on other planets.

____ 7. Life is short, so it's smart to pack in as many experiences as possible.

____ 8. After Adam and Eve's creation, the different human races developed through evolution.

____ 9. If you love someone as perfectly as possible, eventually that person will love you back.

____ 10. Money is the root of all evil.

____ 11. It might be possible to die and be reborn as another person.

____ 12. The goal of life is to be as happy as possible.

____ 13. Love is out there somewhere for you; you just have to be patient and wait for it.

____ 14. Your mother had at least one wonderful kid.

A little tougher than you thought? Face it: Sometimes it's tough to pick through what's hogwash and what isn't. As a matter of fact, millions of fine people spend their lives being deceived with baloney. So how do you break through to the truth?

THREE ANTI-BALONEY PRINCIPLES

Check out the horse's mouth is Anti-Baloney Principle #1. "The horse's mouth" is a strange old saying which means "the original speaker." The idea is when you hear a rumor, go to the horse's mouth to get the truth. If you hear that somebody said that somebody else said that you're a closet Petrobrusian, you track down the somebody else and nose-to-nose ask what was said and why. But what if the horse's mouth—the originator of the input—isn't available? Go to Principle #2.

Get the facts is Principle #2, another baloney-buster. It's amazing what a little detective work can do to guide you toward what's true. You hear that the Navy pays high school grads $50,000 a year to cruise the French Riviera. Before you sign your life away, check the factual fine print at your local recruiter's office. You read that pureed eggplant and liver paste in tomato sauce will cure zits. Check out the facts in several (don't buy what one source alone says) nutrition books at the library. Your friends say a girl probably won't get pregnant the first time she has sex. Check the statistics at any doctor's office. Study the facts.

Christians are getting famous for not checking facts. We seem to get so excited by sensational incidents and so paranoid at distressing developments that—at least in my circles—we've got a pretty solid reputation as head-in-the-clouds baloney believers.

For instance, several years ago a story was told that during a computer check of scheduling for the U.S. space program, programmers were puzzled to discover that planet alignments didn't correspond to the time sequence of history. Somehow a day in history was missing. Well, as the story went, there happened to be a Christian in the computer lab, and he piped up with the fact that when God made the sun stand still for Joshua, history lost a day! When later another slice of time was unaccounted for, the Christian explained that God made the sun alter 15 degrees for Hezekiah.

The tale began on the eastern coast of the U.S., and, as often happens, was picked up by preacher after preacher and speaker after speaker. I saw it in no less than three Christian magazines and heard it probably a dozen times. So I checked it out. Guess what? No truth to it at all. It was 100 percent baloney.

Even now as I'm writing, several years' worth of mail from well-meaning Christians is filling rooms at the U.S. Federal Communications Commission. The mail urges the FCC to deny a request by atheist Madeline

Murray O'Hair to ban religious broadcasting. O'Hair never submitted any such "request" through the necessary legal channels, and the FCC has no intention of banning religious broadcasting. But the panic persists as Christians believe the baloney and pass it on to others.

How many times has the "name of God been blasphemed among [non-Christians]" (Romans 2:24) because of Christians' ignorance of the facts? Do the cause of Christ a real favor; become a thinking Christian and study the facts. But what about input that can't be verified by looking up the facts?

Anti-baloney Principle #3 is: Go by the Book. Most of the important stuff you hear, read, and see about life can't be confirmed by going to the horse's mouth or the greatest library on earth. Look back over questions 1, 3, 5-14 in the True-or-Baloney Test. There's not a person or fact sheet that can give you absolute, definite answers on these questions. So when you hit this level of input, it's time to check with Somebody who knows everything—all about values, relationships, fulfillment, truth, and all that vague, wonderful stuff of life. See what God says in the Bible.

HIS WORD IS TRUTH
Going by the Book will take some real study since God doesn't seem to go for easy answers. It took me years to get over my frustration with the way He "organized" His Word. (Good thought project for you: Why isn't the Bible arranged topically?) My hours and hours of study have paid off in my confidence that God always tells me the truth. It's one of the best things about God. He is as good as His Word. "God is not a man, that He should lie. . . . Has He said, and will He not do it? Or has He spoken, and will He not make it good?" (Numbers 23:19).

Why does anybody lie? For a few days I asked everybody I met why people lie. Some hit me with purses as if I'd accused *them* of lying, others said it was none of my business, but most people said humans lie because they're trying to get out of trouble, excuse their failures, avoid embarrassment, get something, hurt someone, or protect someone. Think through that list. Is there any reason God needs to lie?

So trust Him. Trust what He says to be true:

▶ "The Lord, the Lord God, compassionate and gracious, slow to anger, and abounding in loving-kindness and truth" (Exodus 34:6).

▶ "The truth of the Lord is everlasting" (Psalm 117:2).

▶ "All thy commandments are truth" (Psalm 119:151).

▶ "I will reveal to them an abundance of peace and truth" (Jeremiah 33:6).

▶ "And the Word became flesh [Jesus] . . ., full of grace and truth. . . . Grace and truth were realized through Jesus Christ" (John 1:14, 17). "The Spirit of truth . . . will guide you into all the truth" (John 16:13).

▶ "You have heard Him and have been taught in Him, just as truth is in Jesus" (Ephesians 4:21).

▶ "The Spirit is the truth" (1 John 5:7).

You get the drift. "Be diligent to present yourself approved to God as a workman who does not need to be ashamed [or taken in by baloney], handling accurately the word of truth" (2 Timothy 2:15; see also Ephesians 1:13, Colossians 1:5, and James 1:18).

CHECK YOUR BALONEY BALANCE

See how well you did on the True-or-Baloney Test. Answers of "false" for questions 2 and 4 can be verified in various history books or research articles on sex. For answers on the other questions, work through the following Bible study.

Question #1. See Matthew 5:43-44 and John 15:12. Real love doesn't hit you as if it's a *thing*. Even guy-girl love is something you *decide* to do.

Question #3. Read Psalm 73:2-14, 2 Timothy 3:12, and 1 John 3:13. Would the statement be true if it were "The *after*life is better to a good person . . ."? See Psalm 9:16-18, 73:17-20, and Proverbs 11:18-21.

Question #5. Review Genesis 1:27 and Numbers 23:19.

Question #6. God knows His universe (Job 38 and 39), yet He doesn't mention outer-space life in the Book. On the other hand, He nowhere states that animals, humans, and angels are His only creatures in the universe. Read Ezekiel 1:4-14 to get an idea of how strange some of God's creatures can be. We can't presume that there is no life anywhere else in the universe.

Question #7. See Psalm 90:10 as this statement relates to life *on earth*. How long will everybody actually exist? Remember our exercise in chapter two? See John 6:51 or Matthew 25:46.

Question #8. Reread Genesis 1:27.

Question #9. Think through some responses even perfect love got. Matthew 9:35-36 and Acts 2:22-23.

Question #10. Read it correctly: 1 Timothy 6:10.

Question #11. See Hebrews 9:27.

Question #12. What's *the* goal of life? See Romans 8:29.

Question #13. Review answer #1; think about 2 John 6. Love isn't a happening you wait for. You *make* it happen by being loving even before feelings of attraction hit.

Question #14. It's you! No baloney. Read Psalm 139:13-14, remembering that God always tells you the truth.

9

I wandered into the psych ward yesterday while I was
visiting a friend in the hospital. The mayonnaise-
colored walls were patched here and there with grey
plaster; paint peeled at the corners. I peeked in
through one of the heavy double-glass doors. "Can't
they get her some furniture or a TV or something—at
least a bed?" I asked the pot-bellied orderly who sat
reading a gossip tabloid at his observation table near
the door.

"Nope. These kind can't have nothing in with 'em
so's they don't hurt 'emself. No bed so they can use the
wire in the spring, no TV so they can dig at the plug.
For their own good." He shuffled his paper and began
reading again. "Name's Ruthie somethin'. Regular
schizo. They're comin' any minute to take her to her
court hearing. Second time in about three months."

Through the door I could see Ruthie pacing in the
dark blue cell. A mattress, sheet, and pillow were the
only things in the room. A wire-meshed window had
been blackened on the opposite wall. She wore hand-
cuffs and a restraining belt around her waist like a

How to Change
Your Brain

weightlifter. Her hair was curled and greasy, her jeans and T-shirt rumpled. She turned to see me at the door, rushed to it, and banged on the glass. "Help me! Please help me. They're going to kill me! Please!"

"It's okay; it's okay, Ruthie," I said.

She banged on the glass crying for help until the orderly said, "Step away from there, now. You'll just get her upset. She's loony; her mother committed her for her own good. Here's the deputies now, so step back outa the way." He unlocked the door and caught Ruthie by the belt as she lunged for the hallway.

Two grim deputies took her by the arms and picked up her grocery sack of belongings. She whimpered, moved her cuffed, clasped hands up and down, and looked at me a last time before they took her away. "Please," she said. "They're going to kill me."

"It's all right, Ruthie," I said, knowing full well nothing was all right. It was one of those times in my life when I wished I could be God. I'd hold her, magically heal her mind, and let the chains fall away.

That's exactly what God wants for all of us. He aches to restore our minds, so He has "not given us the spirit of fear; but of power, and of love, and of a sound mind" (2 Timothy 1:7, KJV). "Sound mind" is a translation of a Greek word that literally means a "safe" or "salvaged" mind. He loves us, has provided a way to heal us, and has promised that His truth will make us free of the chains of darkened, limited thinking.

THE MOTIVATION

What do you want in life? (Humor me and actually do this little exercise, okay?)

Make three columns on a piece of scratch paper.

1. List what you want under the first column.

2. Why do you want these wants? Jot your reasons for wanting each item in the second column.

3. Now ask why again. In the third column list why you *need* each item. (This is a tough level of soul-searching, so take your time.)

A good rule of thumb for getting at the heart of things is to always ask "why?" at least twice when you're trying to figure something out. (NOT when your father has just told you to clean the parakeet cage, right?) So by the time you hit the third column, you have a good idea of what you really want out of life.

Now. You'll need a little more concentration-time, so sweetly tell your snotty sibling to practice the tuba somewhere else for a few minutes. Relax and imagine the Garden of Eden again. Imagine that God has just finished creating the first human beings. And imagine that one of them is . . . you! Visualize your life in paradise. Is there anything on your third column of wants that wouldn't be fulfilled?

Well, remember that God wants to get you back to the garden, back to the way you were designed to live. If you're a Christian, your dead spirit has been made alive, and you've been reconnected to God. Your sin-marred body will be revamped to be absolutely glorious. So what needs to be worked on in the present to refit you for paradise? Your soul. It's mind-renewal time!

You've got the desire. Do you want to be wiser next year than you are right now? I thought so . . . because, first, I know that if you've stuck with me in our thinking about thinking this far, you must be interested.

Second, you have some deep wants and needs (column #3) that you know can be fulfilled as God restores you to His original design. I think you realize your thinking needs to be paradise-quality for a paradise-quality life, since the way you live is determined by the way you think. So commit yourself to getting wise. You can do it.

Obstacles are no big obstacle if you really want a

renewed mind and a renewed life. Are you dumb?
(Who says so?) Even if you've been labeled as "not
intelligent," you can grow in renewed thinking since it
doesn't require intelligence. It does require Spirit-
control, a Bible, time, and your will.

Can't concentrate? Baloney. You and I both know
that when we're into something we really like or want,
we can concentrate for hours:

▶ Flighty Fred can spend 45 minutes concentrating
on getting one bolt back into his Fiat's fuel pump
which is located conveniently under a brace.

▶ Airhead Annie can memorize every word of a six-
page letter from Danny who moved to Idaho.

▶ Stuck-on-Stella Stella flunks Lit classes because
she "can't concentrate," but can spend three hours
studying her face in the mirror.

We concentrate on what we like to concentrate on,
right? So I'll challenge you. Keep practicing God's
mind-renewal program even if at first you can't concentrate. Eventually you'll like this mind-changing operation so much that you'll be able to concentrate for
hours. Really.

Lazy? Do you feel you don't need to think since
there are all kinds of preachers and Bible teachers to
do the studying and thinking who can tell us what they
find? Yeah, I know how nice it feels to be lazy, but I
also know it's deadly for me to just swallow what
everybody else thinks. I'd end up living out their ideas
in a sort of second-hand life. If you want an easy life,
become a comatose vegetable fed by tubes. If you want
a life the way life was designed, choose to resist the
temptations of time-wasting laziness.

Worried about problems so much that you just can't
think? Follow God's instructions to you (Philippians
4:6), and His peace "shall guard your heart and your
mind in Christ Jesus" (Philippians 4:7).

No time, no place to think? Make time; find a place.

Don't turn on the radio every time you get in the car. Don't wait till you're totally exhausted to go to bed. Leave your headphones off when you jog or bike. Take walks by yourself. Don't watch TV every time you've got nothing to do. Set aside some small block of your life, cut off as much of the bombardment of input as possible, and think. You can do it.

FIRST, BE FILLED WITH THE SPIRIT

Renewed thinking begins with a right relationship with God, since the "fear of the Lord is the beginning of knowledge" and wisdom (Proverbs 1:7; 9:10). Think of this fear of the Lord as your fear of electricity. You enjoy its benefits, but you don't mess with its power.

As Christians who are already related to God, how do we make sure our fellowship is straight with Him? Read 1 John 1:9. Once we've confessed and been forgiven, His Spirit can control us.

Take a break. Right now make sure you're in your new nature, controlled by the Holy Spirit.

Our minds were designed to be enlightened by the Spirit of God, "for the Spirit searches all things, even the depths of God . . . that we might know the things freely given to us by God . . . in words . . . taught by the Spirit, combining spiritual thoughts with spiritual words" (1 Corinthians 2:10-13). He is our link to understanding truth. "The Holy Spirit . . . will teach you all things" (John 14:26) and "will guide you into all the truth" (John 16:13). He'll use the truth to renew our minds and lives.

The Spirit began His renewal operation in us the minute we were saved (Titus 3:5). So it makes sense to keep the process rolling. I won't preach to you on these passages, but I'll trust the Spirit to guide you in thinking them through.

▶ And do not be conformed to this world, but be

transformed by the renewing of your mind (Romans 12:2).

▶ In reference to your former manner of life, . . . lay aside the old self, which is being corrupted in accordance with the lusts of deceit, and . . . be renewed in the spirit of your mind, and put on the new self, which in the likeness of God has been created in righteousness and holiness of the truth (Ephesians 4:22-24).

▶ Do not lie to one another, since you laid aside the old self with its evil practices, and have put on the new self who is being renewed to a true knowledge according to the image of the One who created him (Colossians 3:9-10).

As the Spirit renews our thinking, our lives are transformed (Romans 12:2) from one stage of maturity to another. The Apostle Paul put it this way: "But we all, with unveiled face beholding as in a mirror the glory of the Lord, are being transformed into the same image from glory to glory, just as from the Lord, the Spirit" (2 Corinthians 3:18). A God-reflecting lifestyle doesn't come from trying to act religious like good Sunday School kids. It results automatically when the Spirit renews our minds.

How does He do it? By letting us "behold the glory of the Lord" in "a mirror"! So what's this mirror? Remember this: When God uses a word symbolically in His Word, He'll tell us what the symbol stands for. In this case, check out the mirror metaphor in James 1:23-25.

SECOND, FIND OUT THE TRUTH

You'll find the truth in the mirror that reflects God's glory: "Thy word is truth" (John 17:17). God's Word will flat-out tell us what we need to know. It's "profitable for teaching, for reproof, for correction, for training in righteousness, that the man of God may be adequate, equipped for every good work" (2 Timothy 3:16-17).

The Bible allows us to think new, true thoughts. But we often just use biblical truth rather than think about it. Religiously intoning verses for oratorial effect, skimming for Bible quiz answers, or rattling off whole memorized chapters of the Word isn't the way to let the Spirit use the truth to renew our minds. These things are fine, but they basically only record the Word in our brains.

I knew a kid in high school who would memorize entire books of the New Testament so he could win a prize of a week at statewide church camp—so he could get romantically/sexually involved with girls he'd never have to see again. Skin-level Christians often muddy the truth by endlessly spouting verses out of context ("Oh, my life verse is Ecclesiastes 10:19—'Wine makes life merry, and money is the answer to everything'!").

The Bible is indispensable for searching out the baloney we've recorded in our brains. King David prayed, "Search me, O God, and know my heart; Try me and know my anxious thoughts; and see if there be any hurtful way in me (Psalm 139:23-24). Since the old-nature thoughts we've recorded for years aren't God's thoughts (Isaiah 55:8-9), we have a lot of re-thinking to do. Speculations or guesses at the truth need to be reevaluated according to the truth of the Word: "We are destroying speculations and every lofty thing raised up against the knowledge of God, and we are taking every thought captive to the obedience of Christ" (2 Corinthians 10:5).

Some of those lofty thoughts of baloney are pretty obvious. When I see the headlines on the tabloids at the grocery store checkout stand, it doesn't take hours of Bible study to convince me that tabloid trash is baloney. I saw one today headlined, "Man Cuts Off

Own Head With Chainsaw—And Lives!" Another good one was "Family Flees Talking Bear—'He Told Me to Get Out of the Forestry Service,' Says Husband."

Other bits of baloney we've thought through in old-nature times and stored in our brains are more subtle. Recognize any of these false beliefs that need to be rethought according to the Word?

▶ I have to be good at everything or I'm a loser.

▶ Everybody is supposed to like me.

▶ Anybody who doesn't treat me well is a rotten person.

▶ Unhappiness is caused by bad circumstances; and unless the circumstances change, there's nothing I can do about being unhappy.

▶ It's easier to avoid than to face difficulties and tough responsibilities.

▶ Things that happened in my past cause me to act as I do.

▶ God secretly hates me since He knows everything I do and think.

▶ Christianity is mostly Christian adults wanting me to think and live as they do. It's honestly not as fun as a non-Christian life-style.

Your old brain and my old brain need a good scrubbing with truth. And that's just two of us. Imagine all the old-nature grime in all the heads of all Christians! No wonder it's important that we believers who make up God's church on earth let the Spirit of Christ cleanse our minds with the truth of the Word: "Christ loved the church and gave Himself up for her; that He might sanctify her, having cleansed her by the washing of water with the word, that He might present to Himself the church in all her glory, having no spot or wrinkle or any such thing; but that she should be holy and blameless" (Ephesians 5:25-27). If any of the above false beliefs seem overly familiar, mark them as ideas that you must rethink using God's truth.

THIRD, THINK THE TRUTH

The Sunday School teacher was tearing his thin hair out trying to get his students to think about Bible truths. They couldn't get past answering his every question with a mindless parroting of what they thought they were supposed to say. He decided to throw them off the track with, "Okay. What has fur, four legs, climbs trees and eats nuts?"

No answer. They studied the floor. After a typical, uncomfortable silence, a backrow kid raised his hand. "I think it's a squirrel, sir; but I'll say the answer is 'Jesus.'"

Mindless, brain-level-only exposure to sermons, Sunday School lessons, sacred music, devotions, prayers, and biblical workshops isn't the route to renewed thinking. Unfortunately, it can often be the route to Isaiah 29:13:

> This people draw near with their words
> And honor Me with their lip service,
> But they remove their hearts far from Me,
> And their reverence for Me consists of tradition
> learned by rote [repetition].

It's not enough for your brain to direct your body to look up Bible verses or to sit still in church services. These activities alone won't renew your thinking to change you into a paradise person.

In the promise "You shall know the truth, and the truth shall make you free," (John 8:32), the word "know" in the original Greek (ginosko) means more than just taking in information. It means to understand or to understand completely. In the phrase "those who believe and know the truth" (1 Timothy 4:3), the word "know" (*epiginosko* in Greek) suggests an even deeper involvement in knowing the truth. "To know" in this verse means "to observe, fully perceive, notice attentively, discern, to participate in the truth" *(An Expository Dictionary of New Testament Words* by W.E. Vine, MacDonald Publishing Company).

Are you a Christian who lives in a Christian family, goes to a Christian school and to a good church, has only Christian friends, and participates only in Christian activities? Your brain might be wonderfully saturated with biblical input. But you know that even biblical saturation isn't renewing you if you're not "setting your mind" on these truths. For instance, the input your brain has received from years of seeing and using the numbers and letters on telephones has probably never registered in your mind. Without looking at a telephone, try to draw the dial or pushbutton numbers and letters in correct order. Check your accuracy, remembering that even being surrounded by godly input doesn't necessarily change you inside.

Set your mind on biblical input. Setting your mind on something demands you slow down your brain chatter. So get away from outside distractions when you're ready to think.

Sear it into your thinking: Your transformation into a spectacular, wise you requires renewed thinking, and renewed thinking requires that your mind dwell on biblical truth:

► Those who live according to their sinful nature have their minds set on what that nature desires; but those who live in accordance with the Spirit have their minds set on what the Spirit desires (Romans 8:5, NIV).

► Many walk [as] enemies of the cross of Christ, whose end is destruction, whose god is their appetite, and whose glory is in their shame, who set their minds on earthly things (Philippians 3:18-19).

► Whatever is true, whatever is honorable, . . . let your mind dwell on these things (Philippians 4:8).

► Set your minds and keep them set on what is above—the higher things—not on things that are on the earth (Colossians 3:2, AMP).

▶ Let the word . . . have its home in your hearts and minds and dwell in you in all its richness (Colossians 3:16, AMP).

Setting your mind or letting your mind dwell on something involves your good old will. Just as temptation-input isn't sin unless you decide to embrace the enticement, truth-input isn't renewed thinking unless you decide to dwell on it.

Biblical input isn't just a bunch of words; it's words that mean things. As an act of your will, you have to set your mind on the words to get to their meanings. If the specific meanings are unclear, get help from resources such as a Bible dictionary. (See chapter 11 for a listing of Bible helps.)

Still thinking you're not intelligent enough to handle biblical truth? Trust the Spirit. God promised His Spirit would guide you into truth. Face the decision right now: Do you believe He will guide you or not? (See James 1:5.)

Set your mind by visualizing what the words are saying. Most of your thinking is done in mind pictures or images, so when your senses transfer the word of truth to your brain, let your mind dwell on those words by picturing what they mean.

Let's try it. I'll flip open the Book. OK, I see the sentence "And John's disciples and the Pharisees were fasting." Picture those two groups refusing to eat. Spend a few minutes on the picture, filling in visual details, adding sounds such as conversations or smells you'd encounter if you were in the picture. Imagine you're a disciple of John. How does your stomach feel? How many are there in your group? What are you doing with your hands? How does your robe feel on your shoulders? What color is it? How do your sandals feel on you feet? Are you standing on dirt or stones? Since you're fasting, how does your tongue feel? Do you think the Pharisees feel the way you do—hungry? Look at them; study their robes, their faces. . . .

Do it yourself. Visualize phrase by phrase any verse of Scripture. Even more abstract phrases such as "The peace of God, which passes all understanding" will evoke some kind of mental image that you can dwell on. The more you fill in the sensory images of the words of Scripture, the more the words will mean to you because your will is setting your mind on them. No big deal, right? Right. But face it: Real thinking to know the truth will take time and willpower.

FINALLY, REINFORCE WITH ACTION

Renewed thinking demands a lot from your will. You first must decide to be Spirit-controlled. Next you must choose to read or listen to biblical truth-input. Then you must set your mind on the meaning of that truth. And you guessed it—there's more will activity to come.

Your will activates your renewed thoughts. Renewed thoughts won't take hold in your life unless you decide to act on them. A listener of the Word who isn't also a doer is like Deanne Dudley who stares for two hours in the mirror, walks out her bedroom door, and frowns, "Uh, let's see . . ., do I have red hair? Braces? A pug nose?" The truth you learn by gazing into the mirror of God's Word won't stick with you unless you act on the truth (See James 1:22-25). Acting on truth reinforces your belief in the truth.

**TRUE THOUGHTS,
ATTITUDES AND BELIEFS = ACTIONS**

It's no coincidence that 29 orders to action follow the Romans 12:2 passage on mind renewal; no less than 37 follow the Ephesians 4:23 passage; and 20 follow Colossians 3:10.

This thinking-acting cycle forms the curriculum for God's school of discipleship. Every Christian is a disciple, literally a "follower-learner" of Jesus Christ. We're to learn all the truths the Master Discipler has taught (Matthew 28:20). Then God arranges on-the-job learning situations for us to act out the truth, to practice following "in His steps" (1 Peter 2:21). He wants us to live what is true, not just know it like spiritual eggheads.

For instance, dwelling on the thought that the Spirit can give you patience (Galatians 5:22) guarantees the Master Discipler will "allow" you to practice that truth. You'll get stuck in an elevator or hit all red streetlights when you're late for an appointment. You'll get a visit from Great Aunt Gertie who talks for three hours without stopping to breathe. Your little brother will throw up on your lap on the way to church.

Plan to do something about what you visualized for each truth. Dwell on the truth, then tell somebody what you thought about, act it out, and write it down—in a special notebook, on your mirror or on notes. Each time you read what you've written, you're again acting to reinforce that truth. Pray the truth back to God; say it out loud.

How can your mind be renewed? By exercising your astounding intelligence? Nope. By first becoming a "better" Christian? Nope. You renew your mind by exercising your will to:

▶ be filled with the Spirit,
▶ get input from the Word of God,
▶ think the truth,
▶ and reinforce the truth with some form of action.

Renewed thinking. You can do it because you don't have to be smart to become wise with truth; you just have to have a will. God's Spirit will activate your renewed mind to transform your life—future, present, and past!

10

Remember our basic maxim about thinking? As a person thinks, so he is. You become what you think.

(*Pssst. Hey you.* Yeah, you. Do you really *believe* that? I know I never did as a teenager. I was always told to clean up my wretched mind because if I thought about rock and roll and surfing and girls and fun, I'd inevitably become a sex-crazed, sun-cancered musician-dope fiend. Now, I knew I wouldn't become that kind of an adult, so I tended to disbelieve the whole scheme that you are what you think. Maybe you feel the same way. Since I'm not sure you actually believe "you become what you think," I'll amend the statement for biblical accuracy. Listen this time and believe it.)

You become the way you think.

You won't become a stamp because you think about stamp collecting all the time, or a fish because you're a swim team member. But the way you think about stamps will shape your future. For instance, if you think you will become more and more important the

Renew Your Mind to Change Your Life

bigger your stamp collection gets, that attitude could shape you into an adult who measures his success in life by what he has acquired. Or if you think your swim team is hot stuff and nonswimmers are generally losers, that kind of thinking year after year will shape you into a snob who sneers at anyone outside his own social class or interest group.

Jack Rash, one of my high school classmates, thought that with the threat of nuclear war, corruption in government, and pollution ruining the environment, we weren't going to last very long. He had one of those "Who cares? Why bother?" bumper stickers on his Mustang. He thought studying hard was ridiculous when the whole world was going to blow within ten years. He laughed at kids who mentioned wanting to grow up and get married. His thinking became more and more, "Eat, drink, and get stoned, for tomorrow we're fallout."

Unfortunately for Jack, we haven't blown up yet. Jack's high-school thinking shaped him into an adult programmed for despair. Today he has no skills to earn what he needs since he thought education was a waste of time. He's an old man even though he's young in years because he tried to pack a whole lifetime into a decade. He's burned out and desperate for the world to end.

Is this making sense? Your general thought patterns, the things you find yourself mulling over day after day, make you into who you'll become. Want to be a person who makes a dent in changing the world? Start now thinking about your responsibility for other people. Want to become an adult nobody really cares about? Forget about your responsibilities to others and think only about yourself.

You've got an incredible handle on your own future. "Decree a thing, and it will be established for you" (Job 22:28).

SLIPPING INTO THE FUTURE

You think your way into your future—good or bad. A good future grows in the heads of people with their "minds set on the Spirit" (Romans 8:6). They practice thinking "whatever is true, whatever is honorable, whatever is right, whatever is pure, whatever is lovely, whatever is of good repute," things of excellence and things "worthy of praise" (Philippians 4:8).

A bad-news future grows in the lives of people who let their thoughts dwell on the opposites: lies, decadence, whatever is wrong and unjust, whatever's morally sick, etc.

Take Nigel, for instance. Nigel is one of those guys who seem to attract the "brain" jokes. You know "When God was handing out brains, Nigel thought He said 'pains' so Nigel said, 'No, thank you.'" But Nigel can shape his future into a good one as he concentrates on the truth.

The truth about brains is that God gives you the right level of intelligence for who you are. God personally designed you before you were born (Psalm 139:13-16). If your intelligence is perfectly OK with the most intelligent Being in the universe, it must be just right, regardless of how it compares to others'.

Now, if this is the way Nigel thinks year after year, below-average report card after below-average report card, he's molding a future that's full of self-confidence. On the other hand, Nigel might resent the truth that he wasn't designed to be Joe-"A"-Student. He might decide he's a loser because of low grades. Nigel could easily program himself for a frustrated, insecure, bitter future.

Think the truth. In a few years we'll be launching into the twenty-first century. What's life going to be like for you in 2023? How old will you be? What will you be like? Do you predict a lousy future for yourself because things look a little shabby right now? Not to worry, because the power of renewed, true thinking can shape your future into good stuff. The year 2023 might not be easy for you, but it can be good.

Notice that I said the power of *true* thinking, not the power of positive thinking or possibility thinking or probability thinking or assertive thinking. Look at all those self-help mind games this way: Thinking very hard and very positively about things that aren't the truth is a disappointing process. No matter how positively I think I can eat six dozen chocolate chip cookies in one sitting, it's not going to happen. (Maybe in two sittings.)

You can think, "I'm going to win the next Olympic 100-meter freestyle" until you grow gills. But if you don't have a truly unusual swimming potential, it'll never happen. Sorry to burst your bubble about positive thinking, but I'm delighted to replace the concept with something that's guaranteed to change your future: *thinking the truth*.

So go ahead. Think the truth about things like your appearance or intelligence and change your future to a good one. Don't force yourself into a future of loneliness and frustration by thinking about how your looks or bod or brains don't measure up to others. Instead think about the truth that God designed you, and you can learn to appreciate yourself as a wonderful person. Memorize the truth about yourself by reading Psalm 139:13-16 aloud so many times that you start mumbling it in your sleep.

Don't slip into a future of externals by struggling constantly to get ahead, to prove yourself, to be rich, or even happy. Instead of shooting for outward signs of success and happiness, think about the true goal of your life. God created you in His image to become a glorious person—one who is as wise, strong, loving, and wonderful as Jesus Christ. As a Christian, think through your destiny until it saturates your dreams of the future. Study Romans 8:29-30, 1 Corinthians 15:49, Philippians 3:21, Colossians 3:10, 1 John 3:2.

The way you think about truths like these will change your future.

THE PRESENT AIN'T NO PRESENT

If I could pop up through the page right now and ask, "How ya doin' today?" what would you say? That everything's great? That you really feel rotten or angry? Frustrated? Depressed or frantic or worried or humiliated or just plain sick of the whole deal?

Sometimes there are physiological causes for negative feelings, so it's worth seeing a doctor if every day feels bad. But more often than not, the source for how your day is going is in your head. Agree?

Thoughts about that argument this morning make you feel angry. Thoughts of that brief romantic incident make you smile. Thinking about what you have to face tomorrow is making you a nervous wreck today. Think about it: How you're doing right now is all in your head!

You usually can't custom-order wonderful *circumstances* for your present, right? But you can custom-order wonderful *thoughts* about your present, since how you're doing right now is all in your head.

Imagine it's raining, you're late, and you drive up behind a beat-up old car doing 20 in a 45-mph zone. When you find you can't pass, you grit your teeth, say things under your breath, and make plans on how to run the jerk off the road. When you finally get a chance to pass, you see the slow driver is a young mother with two crying kids and a flat front tire. Instantly everything changes, right? *When you see what's really going on*, you start worrying if she's going to make it wherever she's going, if she has a spare but can't put it on, if the kids are all right. And you feel a twinge of shame that you thought such nasty things about her predicament.

Get the idea? When you realize what's really going on—what's really true—the way you think can change everything about your present circumstances. Renewed thinking can change your "now"—right now!

Let's work through an example of this change-your-present principle.

Kerry Kesey gets more and more frustrated as a 15-year-old who feels boxed in with can't-do-this-and-can't-do-that rules. She can't drive by herself until she's 16. She can't stay out until midnight on weekends because Mommy and Daddy think it's still 1947. She can't sleep in when she feels exhausted because school starts at 8 A.M. She knows she can't eat six Reese's Peanut Butter Cups for lunch every day because within three weeks she'll become Miss Thunder Thighs of the year.

Now, Kerry can think about these restrictions in two ways.

In one way, she can concentrate on the restrictions and think long and hard about how unfair they are to her. With this kind of boxed-in thinking she feels trapped—surrounded on every side.

So what happens when Kerry Kesey focuses her thinking on the irritating restrictions in her life? Right. She finally gets fed up and busts loose with, "We're not gonna take it! No, we ain't gonna take it! We're not gonna take it—anymore!"

What happens next? Kerry discovers that outside the box of restrictions she *had* been living in is another box. And this one's got heavy-duty walls. Nail-studded walls. And the walls close in to squash her freedom even more.

So if Kerry's feeling bad about her life today, getting mad and trying to smash restrictions will get her nowhere. What's the solution?

Remember I said Kerry could think about things in two different ways? Instead of concentrating on the irritating feelings she has about the restrictions, she can think about what's true.

The truth is: As a Christian, you're one of God's "peculiar people" or "people for His own possession" (Titus 2:14). We've already talked about that idea in relation to temptation. "Peculiar" in the Greek is a compound of "to be" and "around"—suggesting you're surrounded by God like a dot is by a circle.

Picture that dot and circle again in relation to hassles and restrictions. Nothing hits you unless it goes through the circle of God's presence around you, right? So the truth is that He *allows* hassles in your life. If you couldn't handle them correctly, He wouldn't let them in. The areas where you feel most hassled—sexual frustrations, teeth-grinding relations with authorities, rules about laziness, etc.—are exactly the areas the Master Discipler wants to teach you the truth about. He uses "trials" to pressure you toward maturity.

In fact, if you decide to believe God about hassles producing maturity, your problems today can actually give you joy:

> Consider it all joy, brethren, when you encounter various trials, knowing that the testing of your faith produces endurance. And let endurance have its perfect result, that you may be perfect and complete, lacking in nothing (James 1:2-4).

So our friend Kerry can renew her thinking about hassles in general. Then she can tackle the specific restrictions she faces.

For instance, Kerry can renew her thinking about parental restrictions. The truth is: Parents aren't perfect. But learning how to respond to their *position* of authority and to relate to them as adults is critical to

Kerry's future relationships (Ephesians 6:1-3). Kerry can say to herself, *I don't agree with the reasons behind a lot of their rules. But there's a give-and-take pendulum in relationships. When I meet a responsibility (like obeying them by being in by 11 o'clock), the pendulum swings to the other side and they feel happy about granting me a privilege (like having friends over any time I want). So getting in at 11 o'clock is worth it.*

The restriction doesn't pinch Kerry anymore. She's learned to handle it because she's thinking the truth about family relationships.

See how it works? Thinking can change the present for Kerry. No, the circumstances themselves don't necessarily change, but thinking can change the way things are *for her.* Thinking about the truth of these restrictions allows Kerry to be free from the restrictions' pressure. The truth makes her free.

COUNT IT ALL JOY

Reread carefully James 1:2-4, whack yourself on the forehead and say, "Oh, yeah! This stuff is *good* for me!" Changing the way you feel about the present by thinking about the truth is the basic principle in:

▶ running windsprints until you vomit but feeling good about it because it's making you physically tougher, stronger, and faster,

▶ smiling insanely when your Algebra II teacher gives extra homework since you know the drag of extra work is good for your long-term preparation for college and careers,

▶ putting up with the snorts and sneezes of a friend because you know sticking by a friend in need strengthens a relationship,

▶ feeling happy to jump out of bed at 5 A.M. once a week for training sessions so you can go on an exciting missions trip to an exotic place like Bunga-bungaland,

▶ saying, "That's enough, right?" to each other when you're on a date and things get physically arousing; knowing that free, guiltless, love-anchored sex in marriage will be worth the wait,

▶ knowing that enduring the weak points of your folks' parenting style is educating you on how—or maybe how not—to parent your future family.

Is today one of "those" days? Change it by thinking about the truth!

THE PAST ISN'T PAST

The old park-bench bum slumped over his jug of Red Mountain, sank farther into his greasy overcoat, and mumbled, "Hot hell's too near, boy. What I done I done; can't go changin' it now."

His name was Arnold, and I spent about two hours one drizzly afternoon talking to him about how the Lord forgives, forgets, and saves from the hell Arnold was expecting any day now. "You can change the past," I said. "God can wipe it clean and you can start all over again." He didn't give me time to explain, but wheezed off the bench and stumbled off, waving me away with "Hot hell's too near, boy. Hot hell's too near. . . ."

I couldn't convince Arnold, but maybe I can convince you: Your past can be changed. See, one of the strange things your brain does is collect every tidbit of your every day. It's been doing that your entire life. So the past is actually a part of you now. Your past is in your head, and by now you should have the idea that you can change what's in your head. You can change your past.

Sometimes it feels that you have no choice about what you're like now or who you'll become in the future because you're just a victim of the past—the genes you've inherited, the environment you grew up in, the mishaps you've endured.

Bret expects to be Caller Number 11 when a radio station says the tenth caller will win a Porsche, because Bret knows he was born before his parents were married, and it makes him feel like a loser. David expects his watch calendar to click to the wrong date every day, because he was physically abused until he was eight, and there's nothing he can do to change that fact. It happened and it warped him. Angie feels miserable most of the time and predicts she'll never marry or have a family because she got stuck in the middle of her parents' divorce. It's done, they'll always be divorced, and family matters will always be a hassle. These things happened, and you can't go back and change them, right?

Not quite.

You build your life on what you think about your past, not on the past itself. For instance, let's say you go to a party. The whole time, you think you look *maahvelous*, so it seems to be a *great* party. Everybody smiles at you. Four hours later you get home and look in the mirror to see something green hanging from your front teeth. *Now* how was the party? Now that you know what really went on, how does it feel that everyone kept smiling at you? The party didn't change, and your teeth didn't change, but your knowledge of the past transformed—for you—everything about that embarrassing party!

Paul felt pretty good about himself and his relationship to his parents until one night when he was 13 he found out he was adopted. His "parents" had never told him and had manufactured stories about his birth. And now Paul plods along as if he's shell-shocked, trying to readjust to the fact that his mother gave him up, that his real father lives in a nearby city, that his adoptive parents lied so carefully. Paul had always felt good and secure about his birth; now he feels disoriented. And the point is this: Paul's discovery about the truth of the past changed the past for him.

Two paraplegics might have experienced the same accident, but one can be a positive overcomer in life and the other a loser—depending on how each thinks of the past. An illegitimate kid can cringe at life because of his past, and another illegitimate kid can enjoy the fact that God wants him alive regardless of why or how or when his parents conceived him.

Old Arnold in the park didn't need to throw himself into eternity without God because of his lousy past. I wish he'd understood that the past has got nothing on you—depending on how you *think* about it. The ultimate example of how the past can be changed is the way God changes our pasts in *His* thinking:

▶ "I will forgive their iniquity, and their sin I will remember no more" (Jeremiah 31:34).

▶ "If we confess our sins, He is faithful and righteous to forgive us our sins and to cleanse us from all unrighteousness" (1 John 1:9).

Joseph was sold by his brothers into slavery, and yet he said to them later, "Do not be grieved or angry with yourselves because you sold me here. . . . It was not you who sent me here, but God" (Genesis 45:8). King David lied, committed adultery and murdered, and yet God could cleanse David's past to give him the reputation of "a man after God's own heart" (Acts 13:22).

The Apostle Paul was a mass murderer. He arranged the executions of probably hundreds of Christians. And yet in a flash (Acts 9:1-8), God could rearrange Paul's life by rearranging Paul's thinking. People whose thinking hadn't changed about Paul's past criticized him, but he responded:

> To me it is a very small thing that I should be examined by you, or by any human court; in fact, I do not even examine myself. I am conscious of nothing against myself. . . . For I consider myself

not in the least inferior to the most eminent apostles. . . . In no respect was I inferior to the most eminent apostles, even though I am a nobody (1 Corinthians 4:3-4; 2 Corinthians 11:5; 12:11).

Paul leaped from a past of being "not fit to be called an apostle, because [he] persecuted the church of God" (1 Corinthians 15:9) to becoming the most influential apostle in the early church.

THE THINK-AND-CHANGE-EVERYTHING FORMULA

Got a lousy future all lined up for yourself? Mulling through an unhappy present? Dragged down by a guilty or scummy past? It's all in your mind. And you can change your mind about your past, present, and future. Here's the formula:

1. Identify the negative influence of your past, present, or future. It might be a past mistake, a hassle you're plagued with, a worry about tomorrow.

2. Find out the *truth* about it in God's Word. The truth will free you from all kinds of restrictive boxes and hassles (John 8:32).

3. Renew your thinking about it. (See the last chapter to review the basics of renewed thinking.

Are you a little worried about step two? Maybe you're convinced that getting a mature grip on life depends on thinking the truth. But you're a bit nervous that you won't be able to find the truth yourself without asking somebody for *their* answers—and they might be full of baloney.

Well, good; I hope you feel that way. Because then you're all primed for the next chapter, where we get to the business of being guided into all truth.

This is where we get down to the nitty-gritty: Are you going to dig for and think the truth? Or are you going to let your parents, Sunday School teacher, minister, denominational headquarters, and Christian authors like me do your thinking—so *we're* the ones who get to be transformed by the renewing of our minds instead of you?

Letting others do your thinking for you is the road to becoming a Christian wimp. When the Lord is looking for warriors to stand for truth and asks "Who will go for us?" many Christians have to say, "Here am I, Lord; send my Sunday School teacher" (see Isaiah 6:8). But I'm expecting better things from you. You're going to overcome the average, wimpy Christian mindset and dedicate yourself to digging for the truth firsthand.

GET HUNGRY
First, realize that you don't have to squint and grimace and groan every time you think you're supposed to sit down to meditate on the truth. It's not like choking

Getting Down to the Truth

down foul-tasting cod-liver-oil iron tablets. Getting into the truth is more like settling down to a charbroiled, marinated chicken breast with a touch of teryaki sauce. When you're hungry, eating is a natural.

World-system attitudes can kill your appetite for truth. In a strange sort of way, you might be a bit leery about getting into the Word so the Holy Spirit can renew your mind. It's like learning how to swim—you get intimidated by people who already know how, you're afraid that you'll get in over your head, you're in a new element that requires skills you haven't yet developed, and at first it's not much fun. These fears often squelch a believer's desire to know the truths that will set him free from the fears!

Two other appetite killers are *negativism* and *ornamentation*. These attitudes can make discovering God's truth as appetizing as snails on the half shell.

Negativism is denying the future in favor of the present. It's Dickie Doper tripping on cocaine because it feels good now even though he knows it'll burn his brain in the future. It's Paula Procrastinator not bothering to return her library books today even though she knows it'll cost her in fines tomorrow, or Norman Nerd skipping curls in weight-training class even though it's the only way he'll ever grow biceps. Bible-study negativism is the attitude that the effort spent meditating now isn't worth the future rewards.

Ornamentation is another problem. Sometimes Christians regard the Book as an ornament to their Christian lifestyle rather than a source of wisdom. The Bible is spread open on doily-covered tables, hauled around under arms, waved from pulpits even when not referred to, flipped open for filling in blanks on Sunday School quarterlies. Christians often forget that the Word is a means of renewed growth, not sacred paper in genuine Morocco, gold-embossed leather.

The truth frees you to be hungry for the Word of

God. Ever feel that the attitudes of fear, negativism, and ornamentation crush your desire to get into the truth of the Word? Renew that kind of thinking with the truth. The truth makes you free from:

▶ Fear. The truth about being intimidated by Bible study is that God doesn't give us a spirit of timidity, but of a sound mind (2 Timothy 1:7). Your fears come from the world system.

▶ Negativism. The truth about the rewards of Bible study is that they're awesome (Joshua 1:7-8, Psalm 1:3) and are well worth the effort. Check back at the beginning of chapter nine to remind yourself that the basic wants of your life will be fulfilled as God renews your mind with His truth.

▶ Ornamentation. The truth about the value of the Book is that these words are *life* (Proverbs 4:20-22). The Bible is the focus of wisdom for solving problems, making decisions, and growing in maturity. God thinks the Book is vital; He commands us to study it carefully (2 Timothy 2:15), not just carry it around to conform at Christian meetings.

Still don't feel hungry for the Word? No problem. Think through the truth: God's Word is spiritual food (Job 23:12; Psalm 119:20, 103; Jeremiah 15:16; Matthew 4:4). Paul often compares its spiritual nutrition to the physical nutrition of milk and meat (1 Corinthians 3:1-2).

When you *haven't* stuffed your physical body with 84 Twinkies, a gallon of Rotgut Beer, French fries, licorice ice cream with enchilada sauce, and six cups of coffee, it's natural that you'd be regularly hungry for good food—if you'd ever tasted good food. When your heart and mind isn't packed with baloney and trash-attitudes, it's natural that you'd be regularly hungry for the spiritual nourishment of the truth—if you'd ever tasted it first in salvation. The Apostle Peter tells you how to be hungry for the Word:

Therefore, putting aside all malice and all guile and hypocrisy and envy and all slander, like new-born babes, long for the pure milk of the word, that by it you may grow in respect to salvation, if you have tasted the kindness of the Lord (1 Peter 2:1-2)

As a body feeds on milk, it grows and eventually gets to chomp into the meaty stuff like chimichangas and barbecued spare ribs and filet mignon. As your spirit feeds on the basic truths of the Word, you grow in the renewing of your mind and are able to take in more and more meaty truths.

If you're an old-codger Christian who has quit eating for awhile, you'll have to get your appetite back by starting again on the basics of the milk of the Word. You might gag on the meat—and I've never heard of a spiritual Heimlich maneuver. So the writer of Hebrews scolds his readers for having become "dull of hearing" when it comes to understanding the truth of the Word:

For though by this time you ought to be teachers, you have need again for someone to teach you the elementary principles of the oracles of God, and you have come to need milk and not solid food. . . . Solid food is for the mature, who because of practice have their senses trained to discern good and evil (Hebrews 5:12,14).

How can you get hungry for the truth of God's Word?

▶ Rethink negativism about getting into the Bible.

▶ Forget about using the Book as some kind of meaningless religious ornament.

▶ Confess the mental and emotional junkfood that fills your mind and the dullness that blunts your understanding.

▶ Then do what comes naturally to a Spirit-filled believer: Feel hungry for the milk and meat of the Word of truth!

IT'S THE REAL THING

Cass slumped on her backpack, stuck her feet out over the cliff of the 10,000-foot gorge in the Sierra Nevadas, and puffed, "So I don't believe the Bible. There are other religious books, you know."

I figured she wanted to get into a heavy theological discussion to prolong the rest break. We still had a 2,000-foot climb into the snow-dotted peaks. "If God made humans, He's no dummy, right?"

"Right," she said. "If He did."

"Just suppose He did," I said. "If He's intelligent, it would make sense that He'd tell us intelligent beings why He made us, right?"

"Guess so," she said.

"So we ought to expect some kind of communiqué from God. Something that claims to be from God. It would have to be a permanent record of what He says so every one of us doesn't have to sit and listen to a booming voice in the sky every day. We'd forget fast what He'd said; we'd mistake some of the words. So humans should expect some kind of *written* communiqué from God, right?"

"Hmmm" was all Cass said.

"There are only three written records that claim to actually be the truth from God Himself. All kinds of other religious writings exist, of course, but these three are the only ones that state they are directly from God."

I could tell Cass was interested; she sat up and nearly knocked her water bottle over the edge. "What are they?"

"The Book of Mormon and a couple related writings

of the Church of the Latter Day Saints, the Koran, and the Bible. I've studied all three—which you ought to do sometime. Obviously if I'm basing my life and future on it, I think the Bible has the right stuff as God's message. The Book of Mormon has some really rough spots as the word of God. For instance, it reports that God designed a boat but forgot to make any opening in it for the people to enter or for them to breathe. I spent a summer as a missionary to the Mormons in Salt Lake City and examined a first edition copy of the Book of Mormon which claims that it was a perfect book when Joseph Smith authored it. Yet the Mormons have made over 12,000 changes to correct its grammar and doctrinal content. It's nice, but it's schlock stuff as an authoritative message from God."

"And the Koran?"

"Interesting if you're a dedicated male chauvinist. Heaven is a paradise where men can use women to satisfy their every passion. Every guy will have a 'spotless virgin, chastely amorous' (*Sura* 56). Women on earth are only possessions, according to the Koran. The whole book was dictated by one guy—Muhammed— who heard it all from the Angel Gabriel. That makes it a little risky since there's no collaboration from other sources that what Muhammed was saying really was from God. The Koran just doesn't have the credentials of a message of truth from the God who made us all male and female, does it?"

Cass shook her head, which forced her world-system-drenched thinking to a wild, new conclusion: If God exists, His expected communication to us *is* the Bible.

THREE GOOD REASONS

The Bible is the Word of God. It doesn't just *contain* the Word of God; it *is* the Word. This seems like a hair-splitter to some people, but to you it's a vital distinction.

If the Book only contains the Word of God here and there, you might meditate on a section that isn't God's truth. You'd be filling your mind with more baloney! If the Book isn't the actual Word of God, you wouldn't know which parts *are* God's truth and which are baloney.

You're too wise to put your faith in some theologian to tell you which passages are true and which aren't, right? So what would you do? You'd end up (as people who say the Bible isn't the very Word of God must end up) by not being able to base your past, present, and future on the truth but on tradition and experience. (See Mark 7:13 and 1 Peter 1:18 on the dangers of religious tradition.)

Let's say you had a friend named Fosdick who promised to tell you every time his dad's pizza place in a city 15 miles away was giving away free pizzas. He tells you they're free tonight, you drive all the way to Fosdick's Pizzaria, and you get a free pizza. Next night he tells you they're free again; so you get a ride only to find the place is closed up tight. He lied. This goes on for several months. Sometimes Fosdick tells the truth and other times he lies.

Tell me: Do you trust Fosdick about free pizzas? Would you trust him to tell you the truth about really important things? After months and years of Fosdick's flaky reports, wouldn't you get tired of driving 15 miles for possible pizza? Apply all that to digging for truth in a Book that's part baloney, and you'll realize why it's so important to recognize the entire Bible as the inspired, authoritative Word of God.

The Bible is inspired, or "breathed out by God" (2 Timothy 3:16). If you do a quick Bible search, you'll see how God guided men through their own personalities to write a perfect record—in the original documents—of God's exact message to man: 2 Samuel 23:2; Jeremiah 1:9; Ezekiel 3:4; 1 Thessalonians 2:13; 2 Peter 1:21.

Books and books have been written on the solid authority of the Bible as the Word of God. We certainly don't have time or space to plow through a good study on this crucial topic, so make it a do-it-yourself project sometime. Check what books your pastor or church library has on the Bible—remembering that even learned scholars can sometimes dish out baloney on very reverent topics, right? Try to track down two especially good books: Josh McDowell's *Evidence That Demands a Verdict* (Here's Life Publishers) and F.F. Bruce's *The New Testament Documents: Are They Reliable?* (InterVarsity Press).

Our English translations are correct representations of the original manuscripts of the Bible. With the more than 25,000 handwritten copies of the Bible available to modern biblical scholars, today's translations of God's Word in English are reliable. Again, this isn't a good spot to launch into a full-fledged discussion of English versions of the Bible. Josh McDowell in *Reasons Skeptics Should Consider Christianity* (Here's Life Publishers) lists guidelines on advantages and disadvantages of various translations available.

For now, just take my word for it that the *New American Standard Bible,* the *New International Version,* the *Modern Language Bible* (also called the *Berkeley Version*), and *King James Version* are wonderful study Bibles since they've been translated from the original Hebrew and Greek on a word-by-word basis. The 6,413 Hebrew words and 4,876 Greek words (translated into about 6,000 different English words) are important because God's truth is given "not in words taught by human wisdom, but in those taught by the Spirit, combining spiritual thoughts with spiritual words" (1 Corinthians 2:13).

Paraphrases are Bible versions which have been translated meaning-by-meaning. Although these are fine for general reading, they're not adequate for word-by-word meditation and study. A popular paraphrase is *The Living Bible*. Some good paraphrases that also attempt to be translations include *The New Testament in Modern English* (J.B. Phillips), and the *New English Bible*.

Some Bible scholars devote their entire lives to tracking every word of God's truth from manuscript to manuscript, codex to translation. Their research is usually pretty eggheadish, but it's a fascinating area of study—and an important one if you don't want to be a wimp when it comes to knowing how you got your Bible. You can be confident about the truth: the Lord's Word is settled forever in heaven (Psalm 119:89), and it's settled right now on earth between the covers of your Bible. It's everything God wants to say to you about why He made you and what it's all about. So dig in.

THE APPROACH

Look, God is more interested in teaching you the truth than you are in learning it, so a key factor in getting into the Word is constant reliance on Him. Make sure you're Spirit-filled, ask for wisdom (James 1:5), maintain a running conversation with Him as you study. ("This sounds crazy, Lord. What do You mean here? Am I missing something? Why did you say that?" Etc.). Remind yourself that these words are God talking to you.

Be expectant and receptive. Be openminded. Don't overlook anything as too obvious or too simple; truth has many levels of meaning. Be faithful. Endurance in digging into truth is like endurance in losing weight, practicing figure skating, maintaining correct posture, or learning German. Remember it'll be a while before the results start showing up. So plan on a long-range habit of meditating on God's renewing Word.

Take your time. Reading the Bible through in six months provides a good overview of the Book, but taking six months to work through Romans 12 would probably result in a deeper renewing of your mind. Your goal isn't a brainfull of Bible trivia. Your goal is to be transformed by the renewing of your mind.

Where you start meditating on the Word is up to you. If you're a "regular" at a church, a "regular" in youth ministry programs, and attend a Christian school or campus club, you've probably already got more Bible input than you can digest, right? The tradition of hitting you with one topic or passage in Sunday School, another in the Sunday morning church service, another in church training, another in the evening service, and another in a midweek Bible study is often mind boggling, not renewing!

Try to keep up with all the biblical input you can, but also concentrate on a problem, passage, question, doubt, or character that's really interesting to you. The Bible helps listed in chapter 12 will give you direction on finding these topics and passages in the Word.

If you're not especially concerned with a topic right now, start by concentrating on what's presented in your Sunday School hour. You'll get plenty of help from your teacher and from materials that go along with the lesson, and you probably attend it more regularly than the other activities that offer biblical input. If all this doesn't apply to you, try starting your mind-renewal program with the New Testament Book of John.

When should you approach the Word? It depends on your own schedule. I always used to feel guilty about not getting up at 4 A.M. to pray and study like a good spiritual giant. Then I realized the truth: *anytime* is a good time to meditate on the Word.

David meditated "day and night" (Psalm 1:2). Moses announced that "these words . . . shall be on your heart; and you shall teach them diligently to your sons and shall talk of them when you sit in your house and when you walk by the way and when you lie down and when you rise up" (Deuteronomy 6:6-7). David said to "meditate in your heart upon your bed, and be still" (Psalm 4:4). Later he writes, "When I remember Thee on my bed, I meditate on Thee in the night watches" (Psalm 63:6).

In other words, anytime day or night is great for renewing your mind with truth. Don't just relegate your mind-renewal program to a little fill-in-the-blanks devotional period. God's truth can saturate your mind all day—and night—long. Why is that possible? Because digging for the truth involves more than opening your Bible and reading. It requires the handy tools you'll find in the next chapter.

12

So, are you ready to plunge in and start digging for the truth?

Where should you begin? What tools will you need for mind-renewal?

Sometimes you're told to read the Bible, maybe on a schedule for reading it through in a year. Other times you're told to study and look up things and answer questions, maybe in a Sunday School workbook. And other times you're told to have daily "quiet times" when you ponder the meanings of a verse or two, perhaps a passage printed at the bottom of a devotional booklet.

Doesn't it make sense to tie together all three methods in your mind-renewal program?

Review quickly the essentials of the mind-renewing process we discussed in Chapter Nine. Then tie it all together in the following exercise. I'll presume you know by now that no renewing will happen unless you make sure you're controlled by the Spirit. Spend a couple minutes talking to the Lord about the basics of 1 John 1:9; then dig in.

Digging Tools

A MIND-RENEWAL WORKOUT

> How blessed is the man who does not walk in the
> counsel of the wicked, nor stand in the path of
> sinners, nor sit in the seat of scoffers! But his
> delight is in the law of the Lord, and in His law
> he meditates day and night. (Psalm 1:1-2)

These three useful steps will help you understand and
apply the message in the above passage:

1. *Observe what it says*. Read the passage slowly out
loud seven times! Seriously! (I'll be counting!)

2. *Interpret what it means*. Usually, you can do this
at the same sitting as Step 1 or at another time. For this
exercise, do it now. Look up every word you don't
clearly and thoroughly understand. Don't overlook the
obvious. For instance, do you honestly know what
blessed means?

To find out what things mean, first use a good old
dictionary. Look up *blessed* or *meditate* and jot down
meanings. We'll discuss other helps for interpreting
meanings later. Right now, a great way to test yourself
on whether you know what these verses mean is to
rewrite them in your own words. Find a sheet of paper
and try it.

3. *Apply what this means to you*. This phase of
truth-digging will take you all day and will prep your
mind so you're thinking God's thoughts even during
the night! You'll be meditating "day and night." So far
you've read the passage in the *observation* phase, and
studied its meanings in the *interpretation* phase. And,
so far it's been pretty much just brain activity. Now it's
time to munch over the verse phrase by phrase and
plant the Word in your mind and heart.

Realizing that it might help to close your eyes for
each scene, imagine a detailed mental picture for each
phrase: *How blessed is the man* (Imagine yourself looking blessed.) *who does not walk in the counsel of the*

wicked, (Imagine the faces of a group of wicked people—personal acquaintances if possible, or just faces of notorious badguys. They're yelling advice to you but you just walk away.) *nor stand in the path of sinners,* (Imagine that group hanging around a sidewalk or walkway into some kind of bad-news joint, and you're not standing around with them.) *nor sit in the seat of scoffers* (Imagine them sitting now, thinking they're cool and sneering at people they consider "goody-two-shoes". You're still not joining them.).

But his delight is in the law of the Lord, (Work hard to see yourself looking delighted as you read a Bible.) *and in His law he meditates day* (Imagine the surrounding details as you see yourself deeply rethinking this business of not being part of the hardguy group.) *and night* (Watch yourself stretched out in bed, thinking.).

HOW TO COGAG THE WORD

Incidentally, the Hebew word for "meditate" is *cogag,* a fact which you could have found out yourself by using the Bible helps we'll discuss later. *Cogag* is one of those lovely words that means what it sounds like. It's the activity your baby sister performed out the window driving home from the picnic after eating too much watermelon. It's the word for the action of a cow's stomach when it's time to rechew some of the cud the cow swallowed earlier. It's what you're going to do beginning now: *Cogag!*

Read each phrase of the passage slowly, recalling the mental scene for each. Try to tie the pictures together into a "story."

Now, cover over the first phrase and read the whole passage, making sure you actually *look* at the words of the uncovered phrases. Cover over the first and second phrases and read the whole thing, recalling each scene.

At each reading, cover over another phrase until the whole thing is covered. If you forget a phrase, uncover it and read the words.

Now close your eyes and slowly imagine the mental picture story scene by scene. Do it again, this time saying as best you can the phrase that goes with each scene.

Look back at the passage and read it aloud slowly.

Again think through the visualization, and write the passage out in the original words. Check with the Book to see how you did. Don't panic if a few minor words aren't accurate yet. Give yourself a hefty pat on the back since you've just memorized a classic section of Scripture!

Now feel free to cogag the visualization and its accompanying phrases out of your memory bank every time you think of it the rest of the day. Provide more details for the mental pictures each time you cogag the passage. Run through it again just before you sack out tonight, checking again with the Book to correct the wording in your head. Ask God to let your subconscious mind dwell on the whole concept tonight while you sleep.

If you plow through the effort (it takes your will, remember?) of following those directions, guess what? Even if you don't feel different, your mind is being renewed. Restored. You've just taken a leap in maturity to see things as they really are. You're thinking God's thoughts!

THE MECHANICS

It'll take time to develop skills in renewed thinking of God's Word. You'll learn more "how-to's" as you grow with it. But for now, here are some quickie suggestions on the mechanics of digging for the truth.

In the observation or reading-for-what-it-says phase:

▶ Use a good translation for your mind-renewing meditation; paraphrases are mostly valuable for getting an overview of large sections of Scripture.

▶ Watch for repeated words or phrases; they're usually important.

▶ Notice the relationships of phrases for cause and effect or progression from one point to another or contrast or comparison.

In the interpretation or studying-for-what-it-means phase:

▶ The meaning of the passage will be clearer if you've got a few different translations to consult. Several publishers offer New Testaments or complete Bibles with two to eight translations in one volume.

▶ Don't gauge meanings by verse and chapter divisions, by punctuation, or by capitalizations. All these are *un*inspired and were added by scholars for "clarification."

▶ Look up word meanings in an English dictionary and in what's called an expository dictionary. An expository dictionary sounds intimidating and is often directed toward scholars, but you can handle it! Buy one. I got *Vine's Expository Dictionary of New Testament Words* (MacDonald Publishing Company)—which will take care of most of your definition problems—for about $8.

▶ When you want to better understand the biblical use of a word or phrase, remember that the best commentary on Scripture is Scripture. You can look up other passages that use the word or phrase through the cross-references listed in the margins of most study Bibles. If you don't have a Bible with cross references, beg your rich aunt for one. (Who can resist a teary-eyed teenager pleading for a Bible?)

▶ A concordance will give you a more complete list of other passages using the word or phrase. An exhaustive concordance is a valuable reference tool since it lists every word of the Word in its every usage!

► A topical Bible arranges all the passages on a certain topic in one place and is valuable when you're working on a subject.

► Remember that the context—what surrounds your passage—will usually help you interpret correctly.

► Memorize the little phrase which some people call "The Golden Rule of Interpretation." "When the plain sense of Scripture makes good sense, seek no other sense." In other words, understand the words of the Word literally—to mean just what they say *unless* a literal meaning doesn't make sense. An example is when Jesus announced that people should "eat his flesh" and the dopey Pharisees tried to take it literally (see John 6:51-52).

Remember that certain types of writing use a lot of figurative or nonliteral phrasing. These include poetic (the Psalms, the Song of Solomon, etc.), prophetic (passages in Ezekiel, Revelation, etc.), and parabolic writings (the parables in the New Testament). Generally, when God uses a symbol, He'll define it somewhere in the Word (see "dragon" in Revelation 12:9). When He uses a metaphor or simile—poetic devices that combine two images to enhance the meaning, such as "She's busy as a bee" or "He was a bear of a man"—it's ridiculous to twist the words into literal meanings (see Isaiah 55:12, for example).

► If your brain gets pickled on a meaning, as a *last* resort refer to "the experts"—ministers or scholars who've studied the passage you're working on. Ask your pastor for a list of reliable Bible commentators, and start collecting their word study books.

► On some passages, not even scholarly commentaries will help. So brace yourself: You won't understand *every* truth in the universe. Yes, I know it's a big shock. Don't do as some untaught and unstable Bible students do and *make up* meanings for things you don't yet understand. Peter says the New Testament has "some things hard to understand, which the untaught and unstable distort, as they do also the rest of the Scriptures" (2 Peter 3:16). Remember that although some things seem really foggy now, eventually you'll understand it all (1 Corinthians 13:12).

Here's a rundown of the Bible helps I've mentioned, tools that'll help you interpret the Word:

▶ a good translation Bible with cross-references
▶ several other translations
▶ an English dictionary
▶ an expository dictionary
▶ an exhaustive concordance
▶ a topical Bible
▶ word study commentaries by reliable scholars

Yes, you can probably borrow these from somebody. Yes, you can probably check them out from your church or public library. But seriously consider putting out the bucks in your life-long mind-renewal program and buy your own. You're worth the investment!

PHASE THREE TIPS

In the application or meditating on what it means to me phase:

▶ Always visualize yourself involved in the passage. It's critical to see that God's words apply to you personally.

▶ Remember that meditation takes practice. It'll get better, richer. Some passages are easier to meditate on than others, but remember, even in the tough ones, all of King David's excitement about meditating came from working through the only Word he had—the "dry" laws of the Pentateuch!

▶ Be wise in applying Scripture according to context. You know the story of the helter-skelter Christian looking for God's direction by flipping open the Book and directly applying the first thing he saw. The first flip turned up "And Judas went out and hanged himself"; and the second revealed "Go thou and do likewise"! Watch the context for whether you apply the specific truth directly or indirectly by learning a general lesson.

How do you know whether a passage applies to you directly or indirectly? Just follow these guidelines.

Apply directly if you're meditating on *a New Testament teaching or command* such as "Don't be conformed to the world" (Romans 12:2). You're a New Testament believer, so do what it says.

Apply directly if you're studying *a testimony, prayer or reflection* such as "My refuge and my fortress, my God, in whom I trust" (Psalm 91:2). Join with the writer to express those same thoughts to God.

Apply indirectly if you're into a passage of *history*. Remember the Bible accurately records one-time miracles, unique events, mistakes, and even evil. Although Noah built an ark, Solomon married a thousand spouses, and Peter walked on water, it doesn't mean *you* are supposed to do the same. These aren't biblical doctrines or teachings, "These things happened to them as an example, and they were written for our instruction" (1 Corinthians 10:11). Be careful when somebody points to an event recorded in the Bible and insists that that is what *you* should experience too.

Apply indirectly if you're studying the *Old Testament laws and rituals* such as "You shall not wear a material mixed of wool and linen together" (Deuteronomy 22:11). Remember that you're a New Testament person. You were "released from the law . . . so that [you] serve in newness of the Spirit and not in oldness of the letter" (Romans 7:6. See also Acts 13:39, Romans 7:1-5; 10:4).

Apply indirectly if you're working on a section of *prophecy*. Steer clear of applying the passage as if it were an astrological forecast of today's events. I've heard the characteristics of the Beast in Revelation applied to the emperor of Japan, Henry Kissinger, and the U.S. Pentagon central computer. I've heard the "wheel within a wheel" vision of Ezekiel applied to today's sightings of unidentified flying objects. So UFO's *must* be God's messengers, right? Baloney.

Play down the sensationalism and paranoia of prophetic applications and instead apply prophetic passages as motivation to straighten up your *personal* life: "Since all these things are to [happen], what sort of people ought you to be in holy conduct and godliness, looking for and hastening the coming of the day of God. . . . Since you look for these things, be diligent to be found by Him in peace, spotless and blameless" (2 Peter 3:11-12, 14).

As you finish meditating on a passage, do something as a result. Keep a notebook and write out the passage or a paraphrase of it. Or write a summary of what you've thought about. Jump up and act out a command in the passage. Set a goal to develop a quality mentioned in the passage. Pray the thoughts back to God. Tell somebody else about the truth you've meditated on. Write a poem or song, or draw your impression of what you've studied. Design a lesson plan as if you were to teach somebody these truths. Volunteer to give a devotional: go ahead and teach somebody. Plan an ad campaign to "sell" that biblical truth. Take any action that might activate your renewed thoughts!

So dig in! You'll be transformed step by step into the image of Christ (2 Corinthians 3:18) as the Spirit renews your mind (Romans 12:2, 2 Corinthians 4:16, Ephesians 4:23). You'll find yourself well on the road to loving "the Lord your God with all your heart, and with all your soul, and with all your mind" (Matthew 22:37).

And that's just the beginning of the results you can expect in your renewed life!

13

The pinewood fire crackles, smoke obscures half of the campers huddled around the firepit, and the stars are like glitter in a black velvet sky. Joe finally gets his nerve up to stand and give a testimony.

"I'm Joe Carnal and this week of camp has been the best time of my life. This time the speakers really convinced me that the lying and lusting and cheating and boozing and stuff I've been doing is really wrong. This year I'm going to go home and live the way I'm supposed to and be a better Christian."

It lasts two weeks. Last year, Joe's vow of straightening up lasted three weeks. It's a cycle that goes on year after year in Joe's life. He lives a slapdash Christianity, gets convicted about it, vows to be better, tries to be better for a while, then falls back into the same old-nature routines. After several cycles, Joe figures that he might as well give up and lie in the same old rut rather than try any more futile and embarrassing vows of reforming.

Sound familiar? (And how do you suppose *I* know about the futility of the cycle so well, eh?)

Think and Grow Wise

Joe Carnal and I and a lot of other Christians often make the mistake of thinking that a changed, godly life comes from good intentions. Sometimes well-meaning speakers cajole you with guilt about all the things you should be doing as a good Christian—witnessing, praying more, studying the Word, attending church, etc. But pressuring yourself to perform godly life patterns without concentrating on true input and renewed thinking will only result in a surface Christianity. You'll end up with a misquote of Romans 12:2, "Be not conformed to this world, but be conformed to the expected Christian lifestyle."

Overemphasis on acting and doing, rather than thinking and being, often suggests that Christianity is no more than a code of behavior. But you and I know that even with sincere intentions of acting better, if nothing has changed inside in our thoughts, attitudes, and beliefs, the change won't last. Real growth involves all three factors of:

TRUE INPUT ◊ RENEWED THINKING ◊ CHANGED LIFE
PATTERNS

THINKING AS A DISCIPLINE

So I challenge you: concentrate on renewing your thinking. Don't be typical, ordinary, petty, trivial. Nobody ever made a mark on the world by thinking like everybody else. Remember that in a materialistic, externally focused world system, "Man shall not live on bread alone. . . ." You're more than a mechanical body, and you've got to feed your spirit with "every word that proceeds out of the mouth of God" (Matthew 4:4).

Thinking isn't a gift; it's a habit. And like any good habit, thinking requires self-discipline. You can, as an act of your all-important will, decide to "set your mind on the things above" (Colossians 3:2).

Get into the habit of setting aside time to simply think. Your friends will decide you've gone off the deep end your parents will get suspicious that you're on drugs. But just get away from all the mass input you're exposed to, and spend time pampering your mind with renewed thinking. Find a topic or problem that really interests you. Find out God's truth about it, then think about it.

Let events in your life motivate you toward renewed thinking. I hadn't really thought much about God's views on psychology until I directed a choir tour during which which a high schooler freaked out over a girl who'd dumped him. I remember running out of a gas station office to one of the trucks where the kid was knocking around a few sponsors, twisting his arm until he quit fighting, and thinking, "I wonder what God thinks about all our psychological problems?" The result was a lot of study in the Word, a lot of thinking, and the book *From Rock Bottom to Mountaintop*.

If something happens in your life, kick back and think about it. If you're consumed with curiosity about sex, find out the truth about it and think. If you're hassled by an inferiority complex, study the truth about yourself in the Word, and spend your thinking time on that topic. If you at first have trouble concentrating on a topic, jot down your ideas in a notebook. The writing will help focus your thoughts.

Get into the habit of thinking about everything. Don't make the input-mania mistake of thinking you can only expose yourself to "sacred" ideas. Read about ideas. Someone has said small minds think about gossip, mediocre minds think about events, and great minds think about ideas.

Incidentally, realize that the input of ideas from TV, movies, radio, sermons, etc. hits you only once as it flies by your senses. It's hard to really think through something if at the same time you're trying to hear the next sentence or watch the next scene.

With reading, you can stop, reread the idea, flip back a page to understand the context better, look up word meanings, come back to read the idea again later, etc. Is it any wonder God chose to record His truth in a Book rather than give it only orally or on videotape? Even in our high-tech world, you've got to get into a solid habit of *reading* about ideas!

Don't passively swallow everything people push on you—even if it sounds good. Even famous Christians will feed you baloney, hinting that being a good Christian means you'll have a popular, painless, and financially successful life. (The *truth* about living a godly life that follows Christ is seen in such verses as John 15:18, 2 Timothy 3:12, and Matthew 8:20.)

Rely on the Spirit to guide you into discerning what's true and what's baloney. Trash the baloney; get into a habit of saying, "That's not true, and it's not going to be part of me."

Think about obvious things, asking yourself "Why?" at least twice to get below superficial understanding. For instance, "Jesus died for our sins" is so obvious it's almost meaningless to the average Christian. *Why* did he have to die? When you think through the truth about that question and come up with an answer, ask yourself "Why?" again. Thinking at least two levels below the obvious will give you some amazingly wise insights.

Get into the habit of asking questions about everything. For instance, it's amazing the wisdom you'll learn about relationships by asking real questions. You say, "How are you?"; she says, "Fine." You say, "Is that true?", and you'll instantly be communicating person-to-person!

A good question will sometimes threaten an insecure

authority figure but will be appreciated by any competent one. (Again, you know I don't mean you should question the authority of authorities, to refuse to obey them. "Go back to class? Why should I?" or "Why should I do what you say?" are the kind of questions that'll bring you grief, not wisdom!)

Ask questions such as "Is that true? How do we know? Why do we always do it that way? Is that idea based on a fact or an opinion? What does that mean? What does the Bible say about it?" Don't expect or settle for easy answers. Peel away cliches, old sayings, and pat answers. Don't settle for what you suspect is baloney.

Get into the habit of deciding that God knows what He's talking about. He's been around. You don't know everything in the universe, and you're hampered by a past of darkened, limited thinking. So when you disagree with the truth you find, give in by faith to God's viewpoint—even if you don't understand it yet. Don't be like the dozens of Christians I know who, when they disagree with God, jump with both feet into experiences that test the truth to see if God made a mistake (see Deuteronomy 6:16).

For example, a girl who didn't like God's idea of obeying governmental authorities (Romans 13:1) is now trying to pay off a $1000 fine since she didn't have a legal, current driver's license when she—without legally required insurance—bashed into another car.

Thinking about doubts—not believing what God has said—can be good motivation to dig for God's truth and practice renewed thinking. If, for instance, you get hit with the common, recurring doubt that maybe God doesn't really exist, find out the truth about your doubt. When you find the truth, keep meditating on that truth to renew your thinking—even if at first your talks with God about the doubt are always, "OK, God; help me to believe this" (see Mark 9:24).

Paul writes that "if in anything you have a different attitude [than God's], God will reveal that also to you" (Philippians 3:15). God doesn't expect us to agree with Him or to never have a doubt, since He knows our thoughts are usually not His thoughts. He *does* expect us to practice the process of renewed thinking, which will eventually shift our thoughts to agree with His truths (Philippians 2:5).

If a doubt you've dealt with prods you over and over, it's probably a good case of temptation. And you know what to do: Make sure you're under Spirit-control (1 John 1:9), and resist Satan (James 4:7).

THE RENEWED YOU

Renewed thinking will renew you. Even your sin-scarred old brain changes as you think. Brain specialist Peter Russell said, "The brain's internal structure is always changing and developing as a result of experience." Researcher Mark Rosenzweig of the University of California has found that learning (versus passive observation) actually increases brain cortex weight. A sound mind contributes to sound health in your body.

But the really remarkable effects of renewed thinking take place in that battleground of your thoughts and desires and attitudes and emotions—in your soul.

It's almost magical how the Spirit can renew the rotted image of God that still hangs on in man (James 3:9), transforming a person from one level of reflecting God's image to another through the Word (2 Corinthians 3:18). God's renewal program for your mind—and therefore your life—will be completed when you are finally "conformed to the image of His Son" (Romans 8:29). You'll be like Jesus Christ (1 John 3:2), who Himself is the "image of the invisible God" (Colossians 1:15). The image of God will be completely restored in you. You'll be able to perfectly think the thoughts of Christ, the thoughts of God. But you're not perfect yet, right?

Even now, in the middle of God's renewing process, we can "have the mind of Christ" (1 Corinthians 2:16) in each area that we allow the Spirit to renew our thinking. We can take on Christlike attitudes (Philippians 2:5). We can actually think God's thoughts!

Think how thinking like God would affect . . . *the Five Big Do's of Christianity*. What's a good Christian supposed to do? Pray, fellowship with other Christians, worship, witness, and read the Bible. If God's thoughts about each of these external actions are at home in your mind, it's like falling off a turnip truck (which is pretty easy to do) to go ahead and *do* them.

When you think like God thinks, prayer becomes an amazing exercise of requesting what you know God wants and watching the answers roll in (see 1 John 5:14-15). Prayer is no longer a chore or game of now-I-lay-me-down-to-sleep. It is, by His Spirit in you, having heart-to-hearts with God on what He's doing in your world (see 1 Corinthians 2:10-11)—even when you don't know what to say (Romans 8:26).

When you think God's thoughts and you bump into other people thinking God's thoughts, your fellowship is like nothing on earth! You and they and God are all on the same wavelength. You can be like-minded (Romans 15:5, Philippians 2:2, 1 Peter 3:8). When you're walking, talking, and thinking in fellowship with God, you'll be in fellowship with everybody else who's in fellowship with God (1 John 1:7)!

When you know the truth about who God is, your worship won't be something to act out in certain places in certain rituals. Your worship will be from your innermost being ("in spirit")' it'll be genuine ("in truth"— John 4:23-24).

Witnessing is a natural expression of what you think when you think God's thoughts. When your brain has recorded truth after truth of God's renewing Word, you won't have to worry when you're put on the spot to say something as a witness for Christ. "Do not become anxious about how or what you should speak in your defense, or what you should say, for the Holy Spirit will teach you in that very hour what you ought to say" (Luke 12:11-12).

If you're persecuted for being a Christian, Christ assures you that He "will give you utterance and wisdom which none of your opponents will be able to resist or refute" (Luke 21:15). As a Spirit-led believer being transformed by the renewing of your mind, you'll learn the wisdom of saying just the right thing (Colossians 4:5-6) in words "taught by the Spirit" (1 Corinthians 2:12-13).

Imagine the fun—and it *is* fun—of using your renewed thoughts to dig deeper into more of God's thoughts. Things start fitting together, applications seem to pop up all over in day-to-day life, and the puzzles of God's plan begin to make sense. When you're thinking God's thoughts, Bible study isn't a pompous obligation; it's a hunger.

Concentrate on renewing your mind with God's thoughts. Then you can quit trying to act like a Christian because of guilt or good intentions or Christian peer pressure or fear. You'll automatically pray, fellowship, worship, witness, and meditate on the Word as expressions of your renewed thinking.

WHAT'S IN IT FOR YOU?

Living your life the way God designed it is *success*. The world system preaches that success comes with money, possessions, and prestige. But you'll have successful contentment because of what you *know* (Philippians 4:11-12), not because of what you have.

The world system says that a big sign of success is

not having to deal with hassles. But you'll enjoy "perfect peace" (Isaiah 26:3 KJV)—a peace characterized by tranquility *in the midst* of stormy hassles—because your mind dwells on God and trusts what He's said.

The world system says that a successful person has to be a little unethical once in a while, but you'll become all you can be without staining your integrity (Joshua 1:8; Psalm 1:2-3; 1 Timothy 4:15).

The world system rationalizes wrongdoing by whining "The devil made me do it," but you'll have power over sin because your thinking mediates on God's Word. "How can a young [person] keep his way pure? By keeping it according to Thy word. Thy word have I treasured in my heart, that I may not sin against Thee" (Psalm 119:9, 11).

Rat-race existence—where you grow up to work, so you can buy things, so you can work to pay for more things—is out of the question for a renewed thinker. God's wisdom promises you *life*, not mere existence: "Let your heart hold fast my words; keep my commandments and *live*" (Proverbs 4:4).

THE ONE-AND-ONLY YOU
Somehow Christians often get the idea Jesus said, "Come unto Me, all you who are weary and heavy laden, and I will make you all the same!" No, it's world-system thinking that leads to conformity (Romans 12:2); and believe me, world-system conformity is one of the most powerful forces at work in Christian circles today.

Being yourself and being creative about it is one of the natural results of renewed biblical thinking. Look at it this way. God designed you as a one-of-a-kind being (Psalm 139:13-16); there's nobody like you. You were raised differently than anyone. Even your brothers or sisters were treated a little bit differently than

you were treated by parents, teachers, friends, etc.
Your experiences are unique. Nobody has ever lived
your life.

As a born-again believer, the Holy Spirit entrusted at
least one spiritual gift to you, with the possibilities of
using the gift(s) in "varieties of ministries" with "varieties of effects" or applications (1 Corinthians 12:4-7).
The Spirit can renew your mind with awesome
thoughts—"things which eye has not seen and ear has
not heard, and which have not entered the heart of
man." You have access to these ideas because "God
revealed them to us through the Spirit" (1 Corinthians
2:9-10).

Now, put that all together. You're an absolutely
unique person through both heredity and environment.
You've been given natural and spiritual capabilities.
You have access to awesome ideas.

If you could simply break free from world-system
conformity enough to be yourself, to "kindle afresh the
gift of God which is in you" (2 Timothy 1:6), and to
think supernatural thoughts, your every act of self-
expression would be original and creative.

Old-nature self-expression is flat, but Spirit-controlled expression of your new-nature thoughts can
mold you into a new Mozart, or da Vinci, or Fulton, or
Kant, or Einstein, for the twenty-first century! Be a
renewed-mind individual; be creative.

There are obviously all kinds of other results possible
when you step into God's plan to restore your mind
and your life to their superb Garden-of-Eden status.
You'll be wise; you'll be amazing.

So plan a life of thinking. The required willpower is
tough, but with the presence of God's Spirit in your
spirit, you're thoroughly equipped to think the wisest
thoughts in the universe. Don't get paranoid about the
flood of false input around you, but do be careful to
guard your heart and mind from dwelling on the trash

that hits you from Satan, the world system, and your own old nature. Don't bother being a man of the TV or a woman of the magazine industry; be a renewed man or woman of *the Word* as you think God's thoughts Dwell on the Word of truth. Be wiser than your teachers—me included! And let me know what you're thinking!

Bill Stearns
Prairie Grove, AR 72753